Paulus Then and Now

A Study of Paul Tillich's Theological World and the Continuing Relevance of His Work

PAULUS THEN AND NOW

A STUDY OF PAUL TILLICH'S THEOLOGICAL WORLD AND THE CONTINUING RELEVANCE OF HIS WORK

by John J. Carey

Mercer University Press / 2002

ISBN 0-86554-681-9 MUP/H531

Paulus: Then and Now.
A Study of Paul Tillich's Theological World
and the Continuing Relevance of His Work
by John J. Carey
Copyright ©2002 Mercer University Press, Macon, Georgia USA
All rights reserved
Printed in the United States of America
First Printing July 2002

Library of Congress Cataloging-in-Publication Data

Carey, John Jesse.
  Paulus then and now : a study of Paul Tillich's theological world
and the continuing relevance of his work / by John J. Carey.
    p. cm.
Includes bibliographical references and index.
  ISBN 0-86554-681-9 (alk. paper)
1. Tillich, Paul, 1886–1965. I. Title.
  BX4827.T53 .C37 2002

2002002665

Contents

DEDICATION

This book is dedicated to
Robert A. Spivey
Walter L. Moore, Jr.
Kenneth B. Orr
Tina Pippin
Charles W. "Bill" Swain

—great friends and colleagues

Preface

This is the fourth of my books—as either author or editor—on Paul Tillich published by Mercer University Press. I appreciate the interest the Press has shown in the relevance of Tillich's thought. Likewise, the North American Paul Tillich Society, with its annual meetings and periodic international conferences, has kept alive the legacy of Tillich's thought and has inspired a new generation of scholars to turn to Tillich for guidance in an ever-changing theological world. I hope this book will be of help to professional scholars and laypersons who are curious as to how Tillich's thought speaks to a new generation.

I am grateful to Timothy Driscoll, archivist at the Andover Library who supervises the Tillich Archive at Harvard, and to Dr. Uve Bredehorn, who supervises the Tillich Archive at the University of Marburg, for assistance that enabled me to prepare appendixes A and B. Doris Lax, secretary of the German Paul Tillich *Gesellschaft*, was most helpful in assisting me to identify some of the current streams of German Tillich scholarship that I discuss in appendix B. My colleague Tina Pippin of the Department of Religious Studies at Agnes Scott College was a constant dialogue partner as most of these chapters were taking shape, and her keen interests in literary theory and postmodernism helped me to focus more clearly on aspects of postmodernism that I have discussed in chapter 8. The administration of Agnes Scott College, particularly President Mary Brown Bullock and Dean Edmund Sheehey, assisted my travels and research with financial support, and I am grateful to both of them.

I finished this manuscript almost simultaneously with my retirement from Agnes Scott College. Since retiring I attended the International Conference on Tillich Studies (sponsored by the North American Paul Tillich Society) in New Harmony, Indiana, in June 1999. Many people do not know that Tillich's ashes are buried there, and that this historic utopian town also has the Paul Tillich Memorial Park. The ambience of New Harmony, and the spirit and intensity of the meeting, reinforced my awareness of Tillich's rich legacy to Christian and philosophical thought. The papers presented at that conference were published in 2001 by

Mercer University Press under the title *Religion in the New Millennium: Theology in the Spirit of Paul Tillich*, edited by Raymond F. Bulman and Frederick J. Parrella.

I would like to thank Susan Dougherty and Bruce Wagner, faculty secretaries at Agnes Scott, for their assistance in the preparation of this manuscript.

Once again it is a pleasure to acknowledge the support of Mrs. Jane Owen and the Robert Blaffer Trust of Houston, Texas, which together have facilitated the publication of this volume.

Memphis, Tennessee   *John J. Carey*

Acknowledgments

Chapter 1 of this book was originally prepared for a *Festschrift* honoring my former colleague at Florida State University, John F. Priest. The *Festschrift* was entitled *Biblical and Humane*, and was edited by Linda Bennett-Elder, David L. Barr, and Elizabeth Struthers Malbon (Atlanta: Scholars Press, 1996). It is reprinted with the permission of Scholar's Press and the editors. Chapters 2, 5, 6, 8, and appendix C were all initially presented to national meetings of the North American Paul Tillich Society. A slightly different version of chapter 4 was originally prepared for the two-volume *Dictionary of Biblical Interpretation*, edited by John H. Hayes (Nashville: Abingdon Press, 1999); the present version has been revised to fit better the format of this book.

An earlier version of chapter 7 was prepared for a Templeton Conference on Science and Religion which was held in Atlanta in October 1997. My first report on the Paul Tillich Archives at Harvard was published in *Theology Today* 32/1 (April 1975) but much has been added and rearranged at the Archives over the years, and appendix A brings the modern scholar up to date on the holdings and arrangements. Incorporation of this earlier material has been authorized by the editors of *Theology Today*.

I am indebted to Muti Farris, Paul Tillich's daughter, for searching family photo albums and allowing us to use previously unpublished photos of her father in this volume.

Introduction

The impact of Paul Tillich's work in contemporary theology is the influence not of a school but of a pervasive presence. —David Tracy

The legacy of Paul Tillich as a Christian theologian and as a philosopher of religion remains with us as we enter a new year and a new millennium. Although Tillich died in 1965, his way of approaching theological and cultural issues still remain viable amid the changing theological climate of the radical theology of the late 1960s, the various liberation theologies of the 1970s, the impact of the ecological theologies and ecofeminism of the 1980s, and the challenge of Postmodernism in the 1990s. To this list of changing interests we should also note the emergence of a new interest in the relationship of religion and science—since 1987 stimulated in large measure by research projects and publications funded by the John M. Templeton Foundation. The changing themes and interests of Christian theology reflect, of course, that all theology is contextual to its historical period and social circumstances.

At one level, Tillich's thought is just as contextual as anyone else's. His life and career have been described by himself and numerous other scholars and do not need to be repeated here. I do, however, provide a brief sketch of his life journey in chapter 1, below. Tillich's German birth in 1886 put him into the debates over World War I (when he served as a chaplain in the army on the Western Front) and the subsequent political and ideological debates about the Weimar Republic. The intense crisis, of course, was the struggle in the 1920s and early 1930s between the socialists and the fascists for the control of the future Germany. The eventual victory of the fascists caused him to be dismissed from his post at the University of Frankfurt in 1933, and led to his coming to America.[1] He was appointed to the faculty of Union Theological Seminary in New York, where he remained until his first retirement in 1956.

We see further contextualization in Tillich's American years after 1933, as he slowly made adjustments to a new land, a new language, and a new culture. He lived through World War II, the Cold War, the Korean War, and the great Protestant growth period of the 1950s. His interests, even while he was completing the three-volume *Systematic Theology*, expanded into art, architecture, depth psychology, health, and peace issues. He has less to say about politics during his American period because of his unfamiliarity with American culture. Some of his illustrations and references in his various works are dated (just as, for example, are Reinhold Niebuhr's in *Moral Man and Immoral Society* and William James in *The Varieties of Religious Experience*), but the range of his interests was encyclopedic, and his gift for analyzing profound and deeply human issues means that his analyses are still very much with us.

I.

Tillich's thought, of course, has drawn much attention over the years. He has been the subject of countless dissertations and of numerous books which have sought to clarify (and even simplify) his perspectives.[2] The

---

[1]This story is recounted by Tillich in his "Intellectual Biography" in Charles W. Kegley, ed., *The Story of Paul Tillich*, 2nd ed. (New York: Pilgrim Press, 1982) 12-16; and by Wilhelm Pauck and Marion Pauck in their *Paul Tillich: His Life and Thought* (New York: Harper & Row, 1976) 57-138. Tillich's fate is seen in the larger perspective of what was happening in German Universities from 1919 to 1933 by Carl Heinz Ratschow in his *Paul Tillich*, trans. Robert P. Scharlemann (Iowa City IA: University of Iowa for the North American Paul Tillich Society, 1980) 22-27.

[2]Some representative works would include the Pauck and Kegley works cited above, and also James Luther Adams's classic (a revision of his diss., University of Chicago, 1945), *Paul Tillich's Philosophy of Culture, Science, and Religion* (New York: Harper & Row, 1965); Alexander J. McKelway's *The Systematic Theology of Paul Tillich: A Review and Analysis* (Richmond VA: John Knox Press, 1964); Robert P. Scharleman's *Reflection and Doubt in the Thought of Paul Tillich* (New Haven CT: Yale University Press, 1969); David H. Kelsey's *The Fabric of Paul Tillich's Theology*, Yale Publications in Religion 13 (New

North American Paul Tillich Society, founded in 1975, meets annually to hear papers on Tillichs' work and influence.[3] Tillich scholars, on the whole, are not swept away by the current fads of theology and cultural analysis, but like Tillich try to retain a perspective on the big issues of life, death, and destiny. They do not appropriate Tillich uncritically, but they do feel that Tillich still provides us with a place to stand and with a point of view amid current theological controversies. Tillich is one of the few Christian theologians of the last century whose work is able to transcend the contextualation of the years of his life (1886–1965) and to point the way for further theological reflection.[4] Most creative theologians recognize that at the deepest level the questions of theology are more important than our answers.

II.

In this book, I do not attempt to synthesize Tillich's theology or to show all of its ramifications. I do, however, attempt to clarify four foundational aspects of Tillich's thought which in my judgment have not received sufficient attention.[5] Part I helps the reader understand "where

---

Haven CT: Yale University Press, 1967); and John P. Newport's *Paul Tillich*, Makers of the Modern Theological Mind, ed. Bob E. Patterson (Waco TX: Word Books, 1984). A major work, edited by James Luther Adams, William Pauck, and Roger Shinn, *The Thought of Paul Tillich*, was published by Harper & Row in 1985. A most impressive assessment of Tillich is the supplement issue of the *Journal of Religion* 46/1/2 (January 1966): "In Memoriam: Paul Tillich, 1886–1965." This supplement was originally planned as a *Festschrift* for Tillich on the occasion of his final year at Chicago. The interdisciplinary journal *Soundings* published an entire issue on Tillich (69/4 [Winter 1986]), based on papers presented at the 1986 Tillich Centennial at Hope College in Michigan.

[3]The organization and scope of the North American Paul Tillich Society are discussed in appendix C, below.

[4]Some scholars, of course, would make this same claim for Karl Barth, Reinhold Niebuhr, Rudolf Bultmann, Adolf von Harnack, and Teilhard de Chardin, among others.

[5]Of the various themes analyzed in part I, Tillich's engagement with socialism has received the most attention. John R. Stumme's fine study (based on his diss., Union Theological Seminary, New York, 1976), *Socialism in Theological Perspective: A Study of Paul Tillich 1918–1933*, American Academy of Religion

Tillich was coming from," so to speak, as he persued his theological work. Chapters 1–4 clarify his dialectical relationship with Luther and Lutheranism, his debts to Marx in his thinking about history and politics, and his unique perspective on the Bible and biblical authority. These chapters might be seen as "searchlights" on Tillich's life and career.

Part II attempts to show how Tillich's work applies to modern problems. Most of these chapters were originally presented to various national meetings of the North American Paul Tillich Society and the American Academy of Religion. Is *The Courage to Be* still a viable analysis of the human situation? Does Tillich's positive sense of Eros illumine our intense discussions today about human sexuality? Does Postmodernism really dissolve Tillich's major assumptions? Can Tillich contribute to the contemporary discussion in science and religion? How does he look when compared to two other more recent theological writers on creation, namely, Langdon Gilkey and Sallie McFague? Given the paradoxes of Tillich's life, is his ethical theory still viable? The chapters in part II are not exhaustive but I believe exemplify the type of work going on today in Tillich scholarship.

For the convenience of scholars, I have included as appendixes A and B reports on the materials to be found in the Tillich Archives at Harvard and at the University of Marburg in Germany. Primarily for young scholars and lay people I have included as appendix C my banquet address to the North American Paul Tillich Society in Orlando, Florida, in November 1998, since that address discusses the founding of the Society. (After twenty-five years only the "eyewitnesses" can recall how a professional society came into being.)

Some years ago, Krister Stendahl of Harvard Divinity School "canonized" a basic idea regarding biblical studies when he observed that any biblical interpreter must distinguish between "what it meant" and

---

Dissertation Series 21 (Missoula MT: Scholar's Press, 1978), remains the definitive work. See also the articles by James V. Fisher, Walter Bense, and Ronald Stone in John J. Carey, ed., *Tillich Studies: 1975*, Second North American Consultation on Paul Tillich Studies (Tallahassee FL: The Consultation, Department of Religion, Florida State University, 1975) 27-62. Scholars may also wish to consult Eberhard Amelung's Harvard dissertation, "Religious Socialism as an Ideology" (1962), which focuses on Tillich's involvement with a theological perspective on socialism and his ties with the Berlin Kairos Circle.

"what it means."[6] That insight is applicable also to Tillich studies. I hope this book may make a modest contribution to both of these aspects of Tillich scholarship.

---

[6]For example, in his now-classic article "Biblical Theology, Contemporary," in *The Interpreter's Dictionary of the Bible*, ed. George Arthur Buttrick et al. (Nashville: Abingdon Press, 1962) 1:418-32; esp. 419, 430. More recently, see Stendahl's collection of essays, *Meanings: The Bible as Document and as Guide* (Philadelphia: Fortress Press, 1984) esp. 480.

A Photo Album

PAULUS THEN AND NOW

The photographs reproduced here are from the collection of Mutie Tillich Farris. Mutie selected these photos as representative of her father, from student days in Germany to later times in America. Sources are unknown, Mutie remarks, but she identifies some subjects and general time periods as indicated below. These unique "Paulus Then and Now" candids are reproduced here with the gracious permission of Mutie Tillich Farris.

Paul Tillich.
Student days in Germany.
Age: late teens or early 20s.

These two candids—
Tillich alone (left)
and with Hannah (below)—
are from the same general
time period—Tillich in his
30s and/or 40s (?).

Mutie identifies this snapshot as "the family [Tillich with Hannah and Mutie] in Germany before the immigration," that is, before 1933. It appears to be from the same general period as the two photos on the previous page.

* * *

The previous photographs, then, are from Tillich's "German period," up to 1933. The following snapshots are from his "American period."

* * *

With students at Union Theological Seminary, New York.

In Japan, "with the president" (?), Hannah wrote.

Mutie writes:
"In East Hampton
with Leo Lowenthal
& his wife & my son
(born in 1953)
probably two or so
in the picture"
—thus about 1955.

With Susan Sontag.

With Rollo May.

Chapter 1

TILLICH AND LUTHER: A CONSIDERATION OF TILLICH'S DIALECTICAL VIEW OF LUTHER AND LUTHERANISM

In recent years, sparked by the observation in 1983 of the five-hundredth anniversary of Luther's birth, there has been in academic circles considerable interest in analyzing Luther's intellectual and theological legacy for the twentieth century. In that spirit it is interesting to examine Luther's influence on Paul Tillich, a German-born, Lutheran-raised, Protestant theologian who is widely considered as one of the three or four most influential Christian thinkers of the twentieth century. It is both noteworthy and curious that among the voluminous secondary literature on Tillich there has been relatively little work done on Tillich's debts to Luther.[1]

---

[1]Probably the best assessment of these two thinkers remains James Luther Adams's essay, "Paul Tillich on Luther," in *Interpreters of Luther: Essays in Honor of Wilhelm Pauck*, ed. Jaroslav Jan Pelikan (Philadelphia: Fortress Press, 1968) 304-34. Interesting but more marginal for our purposes here is Wilhelm Pauck's essay, "Paul Tillich: Heir of the Nineteenth Century," in Pauck's *From Luther to Tillich: The Reformers and Their Heirs* (San Francisco: Harper & Row, 1984) 152-209. Pauck's book has several insightful chapters on Luther's faith, but the Tillich chapter does not directly compare Luther and Tillich. It is quite helpful, however, in analyzing Tillich's debts to Martin Kähler and to Herman Schafft (1883–1959) and to the moderate Lutheranism that they represented (see 157-68). Of broader interest but also more indirect for our purpose is G. A. Lindbeck, "An Assessment Reassessed: Paul Tillich on the Reformation," *Journal of Religion* 63 (1983): 376-93. In this article, Lindbeck (himself a Lutheran) analyzes Tillich's stress on justification by faith (which he says is at the heart of Tillich's "Protestant Principle") and *sola gratis* as the two key Reformation themes. He indicates, however, that Tillich is indebted to the early Luther and not the later Luther, that Tillich was shaped far more by Luther than Melanchthon, and that Tillich's later developed theology stays within the guidelines of the Augsburg Confession. A sixteen-page bibliography of secondary

Luther is, of course, famous as a church reformer, Bible translator, German nationalist, and as one who spawned a religious community that bears his name. In this essay I am more concerned to reflect on his theological work, both in method and substance, since it is his theological vision that helped to mold Paul Tillich.

I should say at the outset that Tillich was a multifaceted thinker who drew on many sources, and in probing his debts to Luther we do not come to the key that unlocks all of Tillich's theological system. To hold these two thinkers together is, however, an interesting exercise in intellectual history, and I think we will find that Luther is a richer influence on Tillich than has normally been acknowledged in Tillich scholarship. Let us begin this task by sharing some preliminary words about Tillich's life and career.[2]

---

literature of Tillich from 1975 to 1982 prepared by Ellen J. Burns of the Fondran Library at Rice University surfaced several European articles dealing with some later Lutheran responses to challenges posed by Tillich but no articles directly comparing Luther and Tillich. A 1995 computer scan of three databases of secondary literature from 1983 to 1995 revealed no articles dealing directly with Tillich's debts to Luther.

[2]Tillich wrote two autobiographical reflections in his lifetime. The first was written in 1936 (shortly after his arrival in America) and published as part one (trans. N. A. Rasetzki) of Tillich's *The Interpretation of History* (New York/London: Charles Scribner's Sons, 1936). This first autobiography was later revised, newly translated, and published separately as *On the Boundary: An Autobiographical Sketch* (New York: Scribner's, 1966). Tillich's second autobiography, "Autobiographical Reflections," was published in 1952 as an introduction to *The Theology of Paul Tillich*, ed. Charles W. Kegley and Robert Walter Bretall (New York: Macmillan, 1952). Critical treatments of the relationship of Tillich's life and thought are found in Wilhelm Pauck and Marion Pauck, *Paul Tillich: His Life and Thought*, vol. 1, *Life* (New York: Harper & Row, 1976) and in Carl Heinz Ratschow, *Paul Tillich*, trans. Robert P. Scharlemann (Iowa City IA: University of Iowa, for the North American Paul Tillich Society, 1980). Of course many other secondary treatments of Tillich's thought are available.

INTRODUCTION

Tillich was born August 20, 1886, in the village of Starzeddel in the district of Gubenme, Germany, which is now part of Poland. His father was a Lutheran pastor and diocesan superintendent of the Prussian Territorial Church. Tillich studied at the Humanistic Gymnasium in Konigsberg-Neumann and subsequently in Berlin. He began his theological studies at the University of Berlin in 1904 and read widely in philosophy as well as in theology. He attended lectures in theology at the University of Halle from 1905 to 1907, where he came under the influence of the distinguished German theologian Martin Kähler. In 1910 he received his doctorate of Philosophy from the University of Breslau and in 1912 his licentiate in Theology from the University of Halle. For each degree he wrote a dissertation dealing with aspects of Schelling's philosophy of religion. He was ordained a minister of the Evangelical Lutheran Church in Berlin on August 18, 1912, and spent the next two years as an assistant pastor in a working-class section of Berlin. He served as a chaplain in the German army on the Western Front from 1914 to 1918 and received the Iron Cross for courageous service to the wounded and the dying.

After World War I, Tillich accepted an appointment as a *privatdocent* in Theology at the University of Berlin and stayed there until 1924 when he was appointed as associate professor of Theology at Marburg. In 1925 he accepted an appointment as professor of Philosophy at Dresden and remained there until 1929 when he accepted an appointment at the University of Frankfurt. While at Frankfurt, Tillich became engaged with other leading philosophers and social scientists in what was known as the "Frankfurt School"[3] and was quite active in the German political scene. From his time in Berlin until 1933 he was active with a small group of religious socialists as they tried to find a middle way between Christian political thought and the Socialists' critique of Western bourgeois culture.

---

[3]For detailed assessments of Tillich's relationship to the Frankfurt School, see T. O"Keeffe, "Tillich and the Frankfurt School," and G. B. Hammond, "Tillich and the Frankfurt Debates about Patriarchy and the Family," in John J. Carey, ed., *Theonomy and Autonomy: Studies in Paul Tillich's Engagement with Modern Culture* (Macon GA: Mercer University Press, 1984) 67-88 and 89-110.

Tillich was dismissed by the Nazis from his position at the University of Frankfurt on April 13, 1933, and in December of the same year he and his family came to America, where he began a second career at Union Theological Seminary in New York City. He stayed at Union until 1956, when upon his retirement he accepted an appointment at Harvard as a university professor. He remained at Harvard until 1962, and following his second retirement, he moved to Chicago where he taught until his death in 1965.

In 1977, Thor Hall of the University of Tennessee sent a questionnaire to 554 American theologians asking them whom they would regard as their "major mentor." Of the people who replied, 123 designated Tillich; he led over such other distinguished theologians as Thomas Aquinas (87), Karl Rahner (78), Karl Barth (76), and Saint Augustine (51). At least in America, therefore, Tillich appears to be the most influential Christian theologian of the twentieth century. If we can understand his relationship to Luther and Lutheranism, it would give us a good window from which to see Luther's legacy to the twentieth century.

TILLICH'S VIEWS ON LUTHER AND LUTHERANISM

As we turn to consider Tillich's views on Luther and Lutheranism, we should note initially that Tillich was not a Luther scholar in any formal sense. Tillich never published anything technical on any facet of Luther's theology. Tillich was a systematic and philosophical theologian, and he tended to appropriate contributions of previous thinkers creatively and adapt their insights into his own system of thought. This is not an uncommon practice with contemporary theologians, but we should be mindful of this tendency as we begin our consideration of Tillich's debts to Luther.

It is clear, however, that Tillich recognized that he himself had been deeply molded by the Lutheran tradition. In his first autobiographical essay he wrote:

> I, myself, belong to Lutheranism by birth, education, religious experience, and theological reflection. I have never stood on the borders of Lutheranism and Calvinism. . . . The substance of my religion is and

remains Lutheran. . . . Not only my theological, but also my philosophical thinking expresses the Lutheran substance.[4]

Secondly, Tillich's teachers were predominantly Lutherans: Martin
Kähler, Ernst Troeltsch, and Adolf Von Harnack all stood in the Lutheran
tradition, although they had their quarrels with the Evangelical Church of
Prussia. Many of Tillich's formative philosophical mentors (Hegel, Kierkegaard, Schelling) were Lutherans and also lived in considerable tension
with the church. There was a sense, at least, in which Lutheranism was
as natural to Tillich as the air he breathed. In his 1952 "Autobiographical
Reflections" Tillich noted that even his romantic appreciation of nature
came from his Lutheran roots.[5]

But what does it mean to stand in the Lutheran tradition? Tillich
noted that this includes a consciousness of the corruptness of existence,
a repudiation of every kind of social utopia, an awareness of the irrational
and demonic nature of existence, an appreciation of the mystical element
in religion, and a rejection of puritanical legalism in private and corporate
life.[6]

Those who know Tillich's thought well recognize how all of these
themes continued to mold his personal as well as theological consciousness. These themes are perhaps best understood when contrasted with
Roman Catholic, Reformed, or free-church viewpoints, but more extended
discussion of these comparisons is beyond the scope of this essay.

It is worth noting that Tillich's dialectical relationship with the
Lutheran tradition was expressed after he came to America. Here he
chose to affiliate with the Evangelical and Reformed Church, a predominantly German Midwestern denomination made up of two streams of
German immigrants. Tillich's close friends, Richard and Reinhold
Niebuhr, both came out of the Evangelical and Reformed tradition, and,
though it expressed a residue of Lutheranism, it also was distinct from the
generally more conservative Lutheran bodies in America. (In 1957, the
Evangelical and Reformed Church joined with the Congregational
churches to form the United Church of Christ.) Although Tillich seldom

---

[4]*The Interpretation of History*, 54.
[5]"Autobiographical Reflections," 5; see n. 2 above.
[6]*On the Boundary*, 74-75.

functioned as a minister, he was ordained and granted ministerial standing in this communion.

How did Tillich understand Luther? Although, as we have noted, Tillich was not a historical theologian, he nevertheless treated Luther in his lectures on the history of Christian thought that he gave at Union Theological Seminary, New York, for the spring semester 1953.[7] Tillich was also quite interested in the phenomenon of Protestantism and discussed Luther in the course of various lectures on Protestantism (many of which were translated and edited by James Luther Adams and published in *The Protestant Era*[8]). In his lectures on Luther in *A History of Christian Thought*, Tillich observed:

> He is one of the few great prophets of the Christian Church and his greatness is overwhelming. . . . He is responsible for the fact that a purified Christianity, a Christianity of the reformation, was able to establish itself on equal terms with the Roman tradition.[9]

Yet another interesting insight about Luther comes from Tillich's essay (1929) on "Protestantism as a Critical and Creative Principle."[10] In

---

[7]These lectures were recorded in shorthand, edited, and published by Peter H. John as *A History of Christian Thought*, "A stenographic transcription of lectures delivered during the spring term, 1953" (Providence RI: P. H. John, 1953; [2]1956). Later Carl E. Braaten edited and indexed the 1953 lectures and, with Braaten's introduction, they were published as *A Complete History of Christian Thought* (New York: Harper & Row, 1960); Braaten's 2nd and rev. ed. appeared as *A History of Christian Thought* (New York: Harper & Row, 1968). Subsequent references to this text are to the Braaten 1968 revised edition. It should be noted, however, that Tillich never approved the publication of these lectures.

[8]Paul Tillich, *The Protestant Era*, trans. and with a concluding essay by James Luther Adams (Chicago: University of Chicago Press, 1948).

[9]*A History of Christian Thought*, 227.

[10]This essay, originally published in a volume edited by Tillich entitled *Protestantismus als Kritik and Gestaltung* (Darmstadt: Reichl, 1929) was translated by James Luther Adams as "Protestantism as a Critical and Creative Principle" and published in Adams's edited volume of Tillich's early German writings, *Political Expectation* (New York: Harper & Row, 1971; repr. as ROSE 1 [Reprints of Scholarly Excellence]: Macon GA: Mercer University Press, 1981). See 10-39 of that volume, esp. 10-18.

that essay Tillich contrasted "rational" and "prophetic" streams of thought in the Western intellectual tradition. Tillich defined the rational stream as critical humanistic, cultural, and scientific analysis. (Such reflection is, of course, essential to thought and culture and most of what we know as scholarship in the humanities and philosophical dialogue would be in this category.) Prophetic criticism, however, is the kind of perception that goes beyond all intellectual and social forms to the realm of existence and spirit; it transcends all human works and achievements. It is the kind of insight and criticism that critiques human thought and institutions "through the unapproachable fire of the divine majesty." Tillich argued that this prophetic criticism has appeared only three times in the history of the Judeo-Christian tradition: (1) among prophets of the Hebrew Bible who stood against Hebrew nationalism; (2) in the apostle Paul, who stood against the moralistic claims of a religion of law; and (3) in Luther, who stood against the hierarchy, power, and sacramental structure of the medieval church.

Tillich understood Luther as an exemplar of courage and heart. He was one who lived in a "boundary situation" in response to his conscience and held to the authority of scripture over against the claims of all religious institutions. As such, Tillich felt that Luther was a unique instrument of the power of God and one of the great benchmarks in the history of Christian thought. Tillich was aware, however, that Luther's greatness was limited by some of his personal traits, his temperament, the medieval ethos in which Luther lived, and the general acrimony of the sixteenth century. As far as Tillich was concerned, therefore, Luther has to be seen contextually and appropriated selectively in order to speak to the modern period.

When Karl Holl's famous book on Luther appeared in 1922, Tillich reviewed the volume and took issue with Holl's thesis that Luther belonged to the Middle Ages. Tillich said, by contrast, that Luther "belongs neither to the Middle Ages nor to the modern period, but to the great entirely unique period between 1250 and 1750 for which he represents the turning point and the high point."[11]

---

[11]See his essay, "Holl's Lutherbuch," in *Vossische Zeitung* no. 381, *Literarissche Umschau* no. 33 (1922) 1. This review is cited by James Luther Adams in his article "Paul Tillich on Luther," 332; see n. 1 above.

Our task in this essay, however, is not just to note Tillich's opinion of Luther or Lutheranism, but rather to trace Luther's influence on Tillich's thought. That is a difficult assignment because of the differences in temperament, orientation, and time between these two thinkers.

DIFFERENCES IN LUTHER AND TILLICH

Luther, reflecting the theological ethics of the sixteenth century, was also profoundly biblical in his worldview and theological orientation. He translated and interpreted the Bible before the advent of modern biblical criticism; he interpreted the "Old Testament" (particularly the Psalms) from a Christological viewpoint and in general was steeped in the Ptolemaic cosmos. Luther was also an activist in the political and ecclesiastical turmoils of his time; one reason Luther never produced a systematic theology is that he was always engaged in responding to the immediate issues of his times. This diversity in the corpus of Luther's writing helps explain why so many people have found so many different things in his writings and why he lends himself to such different types of interpretation. We should also note that if Luther were to be on the scene today, he would definitely be a seminary man and churchman, not a university man in the modern sense.

Tillich, by contrast, was not primarily a biblical exegete but a philosophical theologian. He was interested in philosophy in a way Luther never was and also was interested in the broader dimensions of culture (art, philosophy, literature, science, and the social sciences) in a way Luther was not. Tillich participated in the new world of North America in a way that Luther, of course, never did. He had to deal with the major threats to Western philosophy and religion posed by Marx and Freud, and all his life he struggled with the questions of doubt, skepticism, and cynicism that had grown out of the history, technology, and secularization of the twentieth century. One might say that Luther assumed what was for Tillich problematic: that is, theistic faith, the authority of the Bible, and the biblical cosmology. Tillich also struggled with questions of Christianity's relationship to other world religions in a way that Luther never did. In the modern North American sense, Tillich more naturally would be a university man than a seminary man.

One way of sharpening these differences is to note that Luther's problems were not Tillich's and vice versa. Luther continually struggled with the question "How can I believe in a merciful God?" Tillich struggled with the question "How can one be a believer in the modern age?" and asked how we can break through the technical reasoning of the twentieth century to cope with the deeper realms of life and faith.

Although in this study we are primarily interested in Tillich's debts to Luther, it is only fair to point out initially that Tillich would reject Luther's view of biblical authority, Luther's method of biblical exegesis, Luther's view of the Jews, Luther's Christology, Luther's view of the church, Luther's political conservatism, Luther's view of church-and-state relations, Luther's attitude towards philosophy, and his attitude toward humanistic learning. For these reasons, I have subtitled this essay "A Consideration of Tillich's Dialectical View of Luther and Lutheranism."

Our task of comparison is further complicated when we recognize that both theologians wrote voluminously, both were powerful and subtle in their thought, both dealt with complex issues, and there is not always a clear one-to-one relationship even when Tillich acknowledges debts to Luther. But the task of comparison is not impossible. Now I wish to consider four areas where I think there are genuine affinities between Luther and Tillich.

THEOLOGICAL METHOD

The issue of theological method needs to be discussed primarily because of the study by Wayne G. Johnson, *Theological Method in Luther and Tillich*.[12] This book was Johnson's doctoral dissertation at the University of Iowa and argues the thesis that there is a general similarity between Luther's theological method and that of Tillich. It is an open question in Luther scholarship whether Luther in fact had a clearly defined theological method. Johnson argues, however, that the key for Luther as a theologian was his understanding of law and gospel. In his lectures on Galatians in 1531, Luther asserted: "The knowledge of this topic, the distinction between law and gospel, is necessary to the highest degree; for it contains a summary of all Christian doctrine."[13] We need to examine in some detail what Luther meant by this relationship of law and gospel.

---

[12]Wayne G. Johnson, *Theological Method in Luther and Tillich: Law-Gospel and Correlation* (Washington DC: University Press of America, 1981).

[13]Cited by Johnson, *Theological Method in Luther and Tillich*, 2.

In brief, Luther understood the "law" to mean the commands of God, both those summarized in the Decalogue and elsewhere in the Pentateuch, but also that natural law of God which Luther felt was broadly written on the minds of all persons everywhere. Luther believed the law had a double use.

The first use of the law is to restrain the wicked in the area of community life, and thereby provide a basis for a sound political order. Luther called this the "civil" use of the law. The civil law is expressed through legal structures and codes, and explains why Luther was such a political conservative. Political authority, which creates and interprets these laws, is therefore deemed by Luther to be part of the plan of God.

The second use of the law is what Luther called the "proper" use, or we might say the "theological" use. Law gives us a knowledge of our sins and shortcomings, and reveals to us that we are guilty before God. The law humbles us and brings us to the point of despair. As such, the law prepares us to hear the good news of the gospel.

Luther felt that if the law terrifies us, the gospel reassures us and gives us hope. The seriousness of our sin, once we grasp that, prepares us to understand the depth of God's goodness and mercy in the divine act of reconciliation. The law and gospel can sometimes be understood as God's "no" and God's "yes"; Luther's word about this has become a classic: "deeper than the no and above it the deep mysterious yes."

This distinction between "law" and "gospel" gave Luther some perspective on diversity of biblical writings and was the perspective from which he measured the authority and significance of different biblical writings. In a theological sense, this distinction sharpened for Luther the difference between sin and grace, between judgment and mercy; and between death and salvation. (It should be clear from this analysis that of all the viewpoints found in Scripture, Luther was essentially a Paulinist in perspective and vocabulary.)[14]

---

[14]This "distinction between law and gospel," and especially of the uses of the law, has generated much discussion in Luther scholarship. A special controversy is related to how much emphasis Luther felt should be placed on the "didactic" or third use of the law. See the discussion of this debate in Johnson, *Theological Method in Luther and Tillich*, 7-8. Further discussion of this point, however, is beyond the scope of this essay.

Tillich took the problem of theological method more seriously than did Luther because he struggled with some ambiguities Luther did not feel. Tillich was also more interested than Luther ever was in the philosophical issues related to the nature of theological language and religious knowledge. In a formal sense, I would argue that Tillich is actually closer to Thomas Aquinas than to Luther in theological method. Tillich frequently argued that the concept of the *analogia entis* (the analogy of being) is the *sine qua non* of any kind of theological language. That is to say, Tillich insisted that unless we can assume there is some broad analogy between human life and the divine life, between human experience and the divine experience, it is not possible to say anything about the mystery or nature of the Divine. That analogy, however, also led Tillich to feel that we can come at the theological task by first analyzing what it means to be human with the confidence that our understanding of the human situation has some affinity with the Divine. Tillich, therefore, began his famous "method of correlation" by asking first what are the basic questions and issues of human life and then followed that with answers that the Christian tradition has towards those questions. In his understanding of the human condition, Tillich actually drew most significantly from existentialist literature and interpreted our humanity around our concepts of fear, selfishness, striving, home, and anxiety. A person who is most profoundly human, said Tillich, always recognizes the edges of despair. We might note in passing that Tillich thought that perception was true for all people, male and female, rich and poor, black and white, east and west, north and south.

What made Tillich a Christian theologian was his assertion that amid the complexities of brokenness, alienation, and estrangement there does appear the reality of "new being"—reunion, reconciliation, newness of life. In his view, that message was exemplified in Jesus as the Christ, whom Tillich liked to call the paradigm of "New Being." Just as Jesus in the quality of his being rose above solitude and estrangement, so, Tillich

---

[Editor's note.] A dated but still important study is that of Carl Ferdinand Wilhelm Walther, *God's No and God's Yes: The Proper Distinction between Law and Gospel* (St. Louis: Concordia, 1973), a condensation of Walther's, *The Proper Distinction between Law and Gospel: Thirty-Nine Evening Lectures*, trans. and ed. by William Herman Theodore Dau, indexed by Ernest Eckhardt (St. Louis: Concordia, 1929).

argued, we also know the experience of new being through the grace of God.[15]

Now the question for us to ask is, What evidence is there that Tillich's method of correlation in fact is similar to (or derives from) Luther's working hypothesis of law and gospel? I do not think Johnson establishes this case in his book, and in his three-volume *Systematic Theology* Tillich never refers to Luther's law-and-gospel scheme. I therefore do not think that formal analysis of the starting point of Luther and Tillich can establish that here Tillich drew significantly from Luther.

There is another way, however, in which there is a distinctive affinity between Luther and Tillich in theological method. Both thinkers, for example, are persuaded that there is a power greater than humanity, which people do encounter in the course of their lifetimes. Both were therefore persuaded that theology is tied to human experience and that in our experience we can know the saving reality of God. Both Tillich and Luther, furthermore, believed that theology is "existential" (that is, it deals with profound issues of life) and that theological discourse finally revolves around matters of ultimate concern. I think therefore, that in the matter of intensity and engagement, we see a distinct similarity between Luther and Tillich. There is no doubt that Luther was an exemplar for Tillich in this way; and that Tillich admired Luther's heart, courage, and passion. One of Luther's famous sayings was that "A theologian is born by living, nay dying and being damned, not by thinking, reading, or speculating" (*Table Talk* [1569] 352). Tillich, in his own way, understood this point of view and in this important way, he stood in the tradition of Martin Luther.

THE CONCEPT OF GOD

In this area, Luther made one of the great breakthroughs in Christian theology by stressing the dynamic activities of God. Luther's understanding of God, of course, has to be seen in the broader context of the medieval church and against many of the assumptions of scholasticism. Luther

---

[15]For a fuller description of how Tillich understood the designation of "New Being," see his sermon "The New Being." in *The New Being* (New York: Scribner's, 1955) 15-24, and his discussion in *Systematic Theology*, vol. 2 (Chicago: University of Chicago Press, 1957) 118-38.

believed that the Western church had developed a theology about the
Divine that was too rational, too amenable to human description, too
confined to theological propositions and institutional definitions. Against
that rational tradition, Luther argued that God is sheer will: God can do
whatever God wants. God acts in everything and through everything. The
theme of God's sovereignity is therefore one that scholars often attribute
to Luther and Calvin. Luther made a major distinction, however, when he
distinguished between God's *absolute* power and God's *ordered* powers.

Luther understood that the basic human sense of God is discerned
within the structures of creation. Through the structures of creation we
receive identity and continuity. We discern rules of law that govern
society, the seasons of nature, and the rhythms and rituals of birth and
death. Against such order and predictability, however, Luther pointed to
the absolute power of God, which he said is "like a threat to those
ordering rules, like in an abyss in which they may be swallowed up at
any moment."[16] There is, Luther insisted, mystery, darkness, and paradox
in the heart of God. God does "strange" work along with his proper
work. This led Luther to feel that there is no final safety in rules and
order, or in rational perceptions of the Divine; we need to recognize that
we are human and not divine, and hence are limited in what we can
perceive and understand.

Luther also spoke of the hidden and revealed qualities of God, which
he called *Deus Absconditus* and *Deus Revelatus*. Luther scholars have
debated at length how to understand this distinction, but on the whole it
appears to me that the theme of God's hiddenness refers to the deep,
mysterious, and ineffable qualities of God. There are dimensions of God
we cannot know, as God works through nature, history, nations, great
persons, and social movements.

Luther's awesome sense of the power of God likewise led him to
repeatedly inveigh against idols. Luther insisted that "God alone is God"
and alone worthy of our ultimate allegiance. Much of Luther's concern
here was, of course, related to practices of the medieval church and

---

[16]Luther elaborated on this point in many of his essays, but the most
sustained theological argument is in his book *On the Bondage of the Will* (1524),
written in response to Erasmus's tract *On the Freedom of the Will* that same
year. See *What Luther Says: An Anthology*, 3 vols., compiled by Ewald M. Plass
(St. Louis: Concordia Publishing House, 1959) 2:551.

claims made for the authority of Rome. In his own way, however, he thereby was a major figure in recovering and emphasizing the sovereignty of God.

The concept of God was likewise a rich area for Tillich (see, for example, his *Systematic Theology*, volume 1) and is obviously an area in which he made a major contribution to twentieth-century theology. Tillich, however, drew on a wide variety of sources as he tried to understand the problem of God. He was indebted to the German idealistic philosopher Friedrich Schelling, to the German mystic Jakob Böhme, and to Georg Hegel as he combined the categories of biblical faith with issues raised by Western philosophy. Tillich felt that one could grasp the mystery of the Divine through the Judeo-Christian tradition and also through various philosophical systems. In his approach to "God language," Tillich was clearly concerned to move beyond the inadequate theistic understandings of God (that is, God as a person or as a being) and to press for a larger and more comprehensive understandings of God. Tillich understood that the biblical concept of transcendence needed to be replaced with more adequate metaphors that can do justice to a scientific understanding of the universe. In his book, *The Courage to Be* (1954), Tillich developed a notion of the "God beyond God" and offered such suggestive metaphors as "God as Being Itself," God as the "Ground of Being," and God as the "Power of Being."[17]

An especially important insight in Tillich's concept of God is the idea of the demonic. Tillich insisted that the Divine contained within itself the element of nonbeing as well as being. This is a relative type of nonbeing as opposed to an absolute type of nonbeing, but is an insight through which Tillich thought one could understand the elements of mystery and depth in the Deity. There is an irrational dimension in the Divine. There is a structural character to evil. In an article written in 1948, which looked back on twenty-two years of his use of this concept, Tillich reflected on how the symbol of "the demonic" applied not only to the Divine but also to his understanding of history:

---

[17]See *The Courage to Be* (New Haven CT: Yale University Press, 1954) 156-90. Implications of these metaphors are also developed in Tillich's *Systematic Theology*, vol. 1 (Chicago: University of Chicago, 1951).

The third concept decisive for my interpretation of history is that of "the demonic." It is one of the forgotten concepts of the New Testament, which, in spite of its tremendous importance to Jesus and the apostles, has become obsolete in modern theology. . . . The idea of the demonic is the mythical expression of a reality that was in the center of Luther's experience as it was in Paul's, namely, the structure, and therefore inescapable, power of evil . . . The powerful symbol of the demonic was everywhere accepted in the sense that we had used it, namely, as a "structure of evil" beyond the moral power of good will, producing social and individual tragedy precisely through the inseparate mixture of good and evil in every human act.[18]

To say this in a different way, the demonic is an inchoate tendency in the essence of God. Tillich felt, by the way, that his thought about the demonic as a component of the Divine was his major contribution to the God-question in the twentieth century.

Where then are the parallels between Luther's understanding of God and Tillich's understanding of God? Tillich felt a clear affinity with Luther concerning the irrational, hidden, mysterious dimension of God. In his lectures on Luther, Tillich stressed that Luther emphasized the *tremendum fascinosum* of the divine majesty, giving it depth, mystery, and a numinous quality. Tillich felt that Luther was one of the few theologians of Christendom who understood the paradox of God and the limits of reason, and that Luther thereby safeguarded the prophetic tradition over against the rational humanists like Erasmus. It was for these reasons that Tillich claimed that "Luther's idea of God is one of the most powerful in the whole history of human and Christian thought."[19]

A related and likewise important debt is what Tillich drew from Luther's theme that "God alone is God." That same motif appears in Tillich as the concept of the "Protestant Principle," whereby he argues that Protestantism as a movement affirms the fundamental dictum that "God alone is God," and that no other person, object, or institution is worthy of our ultimate loyalty. In this way, Tillich felt that Protestantism is a corrective principle to Roman Catholic claims for the church, Orthodox claims for church councils, and Protestant fundamentalist claims for

---

[18]Paul Tillich, "Author's Introduction," in *The Protestant Era*, xvi-xvii.
[19]*A History of Christian Thought*, 247.

the unique authority of Scripture. Protestantism, Tillich maintained, lives
where this principle is vital and has no authenticity where the principle
is weak.[20] I think this is a direct link between Luther and Tillich.

THE HUMAN CONDITION (THE DOCTRINE OF MAN)

The third point of similarity between Luther and Tillich is in their
understanding of the human situation. Both of them stand in the tradition
of Paul and Augustine, which emphasizes the sinful state of humanity. In
Luther's lectures on Galatians and Romans, he underscores that to be a
human being is to be filled with pride, selfishness, disobedience, and
concupisence. This latter trait is often understood as sexual desire but is
more than that; it is an unlimited striving for sex, power, and knowledge.
And Luther felt that concupisence is a cancer in the heart of all people.[21]
These marks of fallenness touch all elements of human life: our reason,
our will, and our emotions. Our fallenness is so total that Luther felt that
we in fact were enslaved by demonic forces. That enslavement leads us
to unbelief, which Luther regarded as "the very essence of sin." It was
this conviction about the total fallenness of the human condition that
prompted Luther to break with Erasmus in their famous dispute over free
will in 1524. Luther thought that Erasmus was "soft" on sin, in the sense
that he believed that our reason was still free enough to make it possible
for us to make free choices to cooperate with God.

It is well known, of course, that Luther thought that in spite of God's
good news of redemption, that we remain in this totally sinful condition
all of our lives. The famous Lutheran expression that we are *simul justus
et peccator* ("simultaneously justified and sinful") did not mean for
Luther that we are fifty percent justified and fifty percent sinful. It meant
rather that we are one hundred percent justified and at the same time one
hundred percent sinful. This, of course, would be another example of
Luther's sense of paradox in theology, but Tillich regarded it as a
profound insight. Luther knew in his own heart that there is a dark side
to human nature and that nothing that we deem reprehensible in others is

---

[20]See the various essays on Protestantism in *The Protestant Era*, 192-233.

[21]This theological assessment, so critical for Luther, indicates that, like all his
sixteenth-century colleagues, he was not sensitive to the differences of gender.
The same criticism of course can be directed at Tillich, four centuries later.

totally alien to ourselves. Luther interpreted Paul's famous discussion in Romans 7 ("the good I would do, I do not, and the very thing I would not do, that is what I do") as being a description of the Christian life. It is as though centuries before Freud, Luther understood something of the dark side of human nature and the mysterious domain of the unconscious.

Tillich, by contrast, developed a vocabulary different from Luther as he analyzed the human situation in volume 2 of his *Systematic Theology*. His bottom-line perspective, however, was very consistent with Luther. Though ideally we are created for fellowship with God, actually in our fallen human state we find ourselves estranged, alienated, racked by unbelief, driven by *hubris* (the drive to elevate ourselves to the form of the divine), and concupiscence. Tillich felt that Freud, with his sense of the libido, and Nietzsche, with his sense of the will to power, both had profound insights into what it is to be a human being.

Estrangement and alienation are realities that touch us collectively as well as individually. They are responsible for the experiences of loneliness, suffering, meaningless, anxiety, and despair that drive us compulsively. This condition, however, is too much for us, argued Tillich, and all persons seek some escape from it through legalism, asceticism, mysticism, and sacramentalism—religious modes of "self-salvation." But what we really need we cannot provide for ourselves. We yearn for renewal, reunion, and reconciliation with ourselves, our neighbors, and with God. That experience is what Tillich called "New Being." It is true that in Tillich's assessment of the human condition he draws heavily on existentialist literature, but his assumption is that only one who is radically honest about the depth of despair in life can understand the meaning of grace and new being. The fact is that new being *does* occur, and we have a model for it in Jesus of Nazareth.

How then can we draw a line from Luther to Tillich concerning the human situation? We have to be cautious at this point. Luther was not the only one to depict the condition of fallen humanity in this way, and Tillich clearly draws on others besides Luther to substantiate the condition of estrangement, alienation, and despair. Tillich also had the advantage of doing his theology after Freud, and he utilized Freudian insights about the unconscious in his analysis of the human situation. Both Luther and Tillich agreed, however, that only the person who knows sin can know grace. Both would agree that only the one who knows sin can know the meaning of forgiveness. Tillich, in his famous sermon "To

Whom Much Is Forgiven"[22] maintained that the one who forgives little loves little. In his lectures on Luther, Tillich noted that Luther alone among the great reformers, "was a depth psychologist in the profoundest way without knowing the methodological research we knew today. Luther saw those things in non-moralistic depths which were lost not only in Calvinist Christianity but to a great extent in Lutheranism as well."[23]

THE CONCEPT OF JUSTIFICATION
(HOW ARE WE "RESTORED" TO GOD?)

All students of the Reformation know this was one of Luther's breakthrough concepts. It was at the heart of his break with Rome. Luther thought that this idea was the heart, the touchstone, the measuring line of all doctrines. In the technical sense it is hard for Luther scholars to know when Luther first came upon this insight. There are some hints in his lectures on the Psalms and also more extended discussions in his lectures on Romans, in the Galatians commentary of 1531, and other academic disputations. Luther's grasp of this concept may have been more rooted in his own experience of dread and anxiety than in his disputes with other medieval theologians.

Briefly put, Luther—drawing heavily on the apostle Paul—felt that our deliverance from sin is a free act of God. As fallen, sinful human beings, we claim no merit or worth; we deserve nothing more than condemnation; but we receive grace through faith. Luther in various ways thought this grace came to us through the suffering of Christ, who through his own suffering made us more aware of our sin, but Luther was convinced that God has acted mysteriously in the event of Christ to restore all of humanity. We are "imputed righteous," as it were, in spite of the fact that we remain sinful. The doctrine of justification is therefore related to a sense of the divine forgiveness and the mercy of God.

An important corollary to stress is that though Luther waxed eloquent on his forgiveness and restoration, he had little sense of sanctification or, as we might say, growth in the religious life. Here is where Luther differed profoundly from Calvin, Thomas Aquinas, John Wesley, and even some of the Anabaptists. We are, in Luther's judgement, sinners and

---

[22]In *The New Being*, 3-14.
[23]*A History of Christian Thought*, 246.

we remain sinners, but we rejoice that God claims us in spite of our sin, and we can live confidently with faith in Christ Jesus. That meant for Luther that though we know we are sinners, we should not be paralyzed by that awareness. Life in the world requires inevitable compromises between unpleasant alternatives and ambigious options. As some interpreters of Luther have said, his theology is as dangerous as it is profound.

Tillich stands very close to Luther on the matter of justification, but again uses a different vocabulary. Tillich talks about the grace that comes totally from the divine initiative. It is a grace that brings about a new creation, a new being; it is the power of transformation. Justification, Tillich noted, is both an act of God and a human experience; it is decisive for the whole Christian message as a salvation from despair about one's guilt.

In an attempt to make this idea more understandable to a twentieth-century audience, Tillich liked to use the word "acceptance" which he drew from the terminology of psychotherapy. In one of his sermons entitled "You Are Accepted," he wrote:

> Grace strikes us when we are in great pain and restlessness. It strikes us when we walk through the dark valley of a meaningless and empty life. It strikes us when we feel that our separation is deeper than usual, because we have violated another life, a life which he loved, from which we were estranged. It strikes us when our disgust for our own being, our indifference, our weakness, our hostility, and our lack of direction and composure have become intolerable to us. It strikes us when year after year the longed-for perfection of life does not appear, when the old compulsions reign within us as they have for decades, when despair destroys all joy and courage. Sometimes at that moment a wave of light breaks into our darkness and it is as though a voice were saying: "You are accepted. *You are accepted*, accepted by that which is greater than you, and the name of which you do not know. Do not ask for the name now; perhaps you will find it later. Do not try to do anything now; perhaps later you will do much. Do not seek for anything; do not perform anything; do not intend anything. *Simply accept the fact that you are accepted!*" If that happens to us, we experience grace. After such an experience we may not be better than before, and we may not believe more than before. But everything is transformed. In that moment, grace conquers sin, and reconciliation bridges the gulf of

estrangement. And nothing is demanded of this experience, no religious
or moral or intellectual presupposition, nothing but *acceptance*.[24]

To summarize the similarities of language and concern about our
being restored and forgiven by God: Luther is more Christ-centered and
traditionally Pauline in his vocabulary. Tillich breaks from the conventional categories and uses psychological language to express this old truth
in a new way. But in theological substance, he again stands very close to
Luther.

CONCLUSION

This study has been a modest analysis of Luther's influence upon a
twentieth-century German-American theologian. Of course the influence
of Luther goes in many ways through the centuries and is felt in
intellectual history, politics, and culture as well as through theology. Yet
by clarifying how Paul Tillich drew on Luther (remember he called
Luther "one of the few great prophets of the Christian church") and
noting how Tillich adapted Luther's ideas, we are reminded that whoever
studies Luther deals not only with sixteenth-century history but also with
continuing insights about God, life, death, and destiny.

I have also tried to clarify in this essay in what ways Tillich stood in
the Lutheran tradition. Although Lutheran by birth and culture and
influenced by Luther on several critical theological points, it is clear that
Tillich was not a typical Lutheran confessional theologian. In some ways
his differences with Luther were as profound as his debts. Though Luther
was for Tillich a giant over a 500-year span of Christian life and thought,
Tillich was also keenly aware of how Luther's ideas were molded by the
parochial framework of the history and culture of his own time. Clearly
Tillich never thought that Luther could simply be "reheated" and
presented to the twentieth century as a viable theological voice. Luther's
insights need reformulation and adaptation to a new social, cultural, and
political climate. Tillich is one model of how this might be done.

There is, however, one more point emerging out of this study for contemporary Tillich scholarship. On the whole, recent Tillich scholarship

---

[24]"You Are Accepted," in *The Shaking of the Foundations* (New York:
Scribner's, 1953) 161-62.

has been much more interested in Tillich's contributions as a theologian of culture than in his work as a systematic theologian.[25] Scholars have tended therefore to probe his relationship to Schelling and Hegel far more than his relationship with Luther or any other major Christian thinker. I hope this study makes clear, however, that whoever would wish to understand Tillich as a theologian needs to look not only to Hegel, Schelling, and Kierkegaard, but also in some special ways to Tillich's lifelong engagement with the reformer of Wittenburg.

---

[25]See, e.g., the various assessments of Tillich offered in my edited books *Kairos and Logos: Studies in the Roots and Implications of Tillich's Theology* (Macon GA: Mercer University Press, 1984) and *Theonomy and Autonomy: Studies in Paul Tillich's Engagement with Modern Culture* (Macon GA: Mercer University Press, 1984).

Chapter 2

TILLICH, MARX, AND THE INTERPRETATION OF HISTORY

That Paul Tillich was interested in the thought of Karl Marx is widely known among Tillich scholars. Tillich's early German writings on socialism, his sympathy for the social critiques of religion, and his efforts to promulgate a religious-socialist movement in Germany are all evidences of his debt to Karl Marx. Tillich was deeply influenced by Marx's critique of capitalism, and he used that critique in his numerous early assessments of capitalism as the basic source of economic injustice in the modern world.[1] What is less well known, even among Tillich scholars, is that Tillich had a lifelong interest in Marx and Marxism. An analysis of both published and unpublished articles right up to Tillich's death in 1965 shows his continuing interest in Marx. Two key articles addressed Marx specifically: a 1948 *Christian Century* article on "How Much Truth Is There in Karl Marx?" and a subsequent piece on "Marx's View of History," in a 1960 *Festschrift* for Paul Radin.[2] To look in depth at Tillich's engagement with Marx is especially revealing for Tillich's understanding of history, and that is what I want to focus on in this essay.[3]

---

[1]These early writings are now accessible in *The Spiritual Situation in Our Technical Society*, ed. and introduced by J. Mark Thomas (Macon GA: Mercer University Press, 1988).

[2]*Culture in History: Essays in Honor of Paul Radin*, ed. Stanley Diamond (New York: Columbia University Press for Brandeis University, 1960; repr.: New York: Octagon Books, 1981).

[3]It must be recognized, of course, that the interpretation of history has important philosophical and theological dimensions which are beyond the scope of this paper. Here I have chosen to focus on the political dimensions of the interpretation of history in Tillch since these facets loom so large in the present dialogue, and Marx's own interest in history is related so inseparably from his political consciousness.

Initially, I will review some of the main themes of Marx's understanding of history, and then will move on to (1) Tillich's appreciation
of Marx; (2) his criticism of Marx's understanding of history; and (3) an
evaluation of this interesting relationship. I undertake this analysis with
two important preliminary observations: first, that Tillich's debt to Marx
is broader than this topic of the meaning of history, and second, that
Tillich's understanding of history is more complex than what is illumined
by this comparison with Marx. With those matters noted, let us begin by
reviewing some of the salient features of Marx's understanding of history.

MARX'S INTERPRETATION OF HISTORY.[4]

In his various writings Marx sought to interpret the unfolding of
human history from an economic perspective. Persons in society find it
necessary to produce certain goods which are indispensable, and the
production of these goods requires that people enter into relationships
with each other. The sum total of these relationships forms the economic
structure of society, and this, in turn, constitutes the real foundation upon
which legal and political superstructures are built. For Marx it is the
mode of production in any given society that determines the general character of the social, political, and spiritual processes of life.[5] The major
epochs (or periods) of history, therefore, are those that are characterized
by different modes of production. For Marx there are four such major
epochs in human history.

(1) *Primitive communism*, which is characteristic of simple societies,
and in which the chief occupations are agriculture and handicrafts, the

---

[4]It must be noted at the outset of this analysis that the concept of history is
perhaps the crucial element behind all facets of Marx's thought, and a thorough
study of this topic would have to treat his concepts of property, modes of
production, values, institutions, and ideology in considerable detail. An extensive
analysis of all these facets of Marx's thought lies beyond the scope of this study.
The following summary will attempt to treat the major facets of Marx's thought,
with special reference to the points Tillich has either appropriated or criticized.
For an extensive study of this topic, see Martin M. Buber, *Karl Marx's
Interpretation of History* (Cambridge MA: Harvard University Press, 1950).

[5]Karl Marx, *A Contribution to the Critique of Political Economy*, trans. N. I.
Stone (Chicago: Charles H. Kerr and Co., 1904) 264-71.

yield from which is divided by the producers. Goods in such societies are produced mainly for consumption, but there is a limited amount of trading between societies.[6]

(2) *(Ancient) Slavery*, which is typified by ancient Greece and Rome, and which marks a transition to civilization. Slave labor produces a surplus of value—that is, slaves are not paid the full worth of their labor, hence a merchant (middle) class begins to emerge. The merchant tends to exploit the producers of goods; he amasses wealth and property, and extends markets. As the power of the merchant class expands, the masses begin to experience poverty.[7]

(3) *Medieval Feudalism*, the system that follows the downfall of slavery, in which the worker owns the means of production, but is a serf, and must pay some form of rent to his lord. There are, however, usurers who are anxious to deprive workers of their money, and a worker's freedom over his production of goods is constantly threatened by unfair systems of taxation and guild organizations.[8]

(4) *Capitalism*, which is the response to expanding markets and the mechanization of industry, and which is noted for its dividing the human community into two distinct classes: the bourgeoisie and the proletariat. Under capitalism the bourgeoisie are the wealthy, the owners of land and the means of production; the proletariat is the working class which is exploited for the sake of profits and markets, and are not paid the full value of their labor.[9] The transition to a capitalistic society Marx saw as taking place in the sixteenth century, but the really demonic element of capitalism became most apparent with the impact of industrialization in the late eighteenth and early nineteenth centuries.

Marx saw the advent of capitalism as the root of the greatest crimes against humanity that the world has ever known. The privileged class creates a political and legal system to sustain their favored position. Working people eventually lose all their freedom, and live their whole

---

[6]*Capital*, vol. 1, trans. Samuel Moore and Edward Aveling (Chicago: Charles H. Kerr and Co., 1906) 89-90.

[7]Engels elaborates on this historical stage in *The Origin of the Family, State, and Property*, trans. Ernest Untermann (Chicago: Charles H. Kerr and Co., 1902) 180-89.

[8]*Capital* 1:822-23.

[9]*Capital* 1:624-25; cf. *The Communist Manifesto*, trans. Samuel Moore (Chicago: Henry Regnery Co., 1954) 13.

lives at the beck and call of their employer.[10] The result of capitalism, however, is that the system more and more eliminates the small craftsman, and society finds itself sharply divided between the privileged and the working classes. Marx's projected solution to the bourgeoisie-proletariat tension is well known: the aggressive privileged class drives more and more people into the ranks of poorly paid workers; the workers grow in strength and class consciousness, until, at the opportune time, they overthrow the greedy privileged power structure and establish a "dictatorship of the proletariat." This dictatorship, however, is only a transitional stage for planning and the consolidation of power; the real goal is the establishment of a classless society, in which all persons will be treated with respect, paid the full value for their labor, and will enjoy peace and security. Under these conditions, there will be no need for the state to control vested power interests nor to suppress revolutionary tendencies, so the state will "wither away."[11]

Around the controlling themes of the mode of production and the class struggle,[12] Marx wove several other important perspectives on history. The movement of history is a result of humanity's struggle for a better social and economic existence. Sidney Hook well summarizes the Marxian position:

> The movement of history is not imposed from without by the creative fiat of an Absolute Mind nor is it the result of a dynamic urge within matter. It develops out of the redirective activity of human beings trying to meet their natural and social needs. Human history may be viewed as a process in which new needs are created as a result of material changes instituted to fulfill the old. According to Marx, the whole of theoretical culture, including science, arises either directly or indirectly as an answer to some social want or lack. The change in the character and quality of human needs, including the means of gratifying them, is the keynote not merely to historical change but to the changes of human nature.[13]

---

[10]*Capital* 1:369-70, 376-77; *The Communist Manifesto*, 16-28.

[11]*The Communist Manifesto*, 28-54, 81-82.

[12]Cf. *The Communist Manifesto*, 13: "The history of all hitherto existing society in the history of class struggles."

[13]Sidney Hook, *From Hegel to Marx: Studies in the Intellectual Development of Karl Marx* (London: V. Gollancz; New York: Reynal & Hitchcock, 1936;

As opposed to Hegel, then, Marx saw the clue to history in the human drives to satisfy needs. The moving powers of history are the concrete, tangible factors of human existence; the strength of these powers is related to the economic situation. It is for this reason that Marx is aptly called a "materialist," in contrast to Hegel's "idealism" (for example, Hegel's famous dictum that "history is God on the march").[14]

This movement of history, however, does not proceed aimlessly. Marx was persuaded that there is a dialectical pattern to the movement of history,[15] and that this pattern can be scientifically studied.[16] Marx maintained that any object, institution, or idea in history (*thesis*) generates an inner hostility against itself (*antithesis*), and the resultant interaction produces a *synthesis*. The pattern is then repeated, with the synthesis becoming a new thesis. Marx found support for this idea in the natural order in the work of Darwin,[17] but felt that its most obvious manifestation

---

various reprints 1936–1994, including: New York: Columbia University Press, 1994) 277-78.

[14]Hegel's view that Spirit (*Geist*) is working itself out and shaping history is developed in his introduction to his *Philosophy of History*. An abridged version of this introduction appears in *Philosophic Classics: From Plato to Nietzsche*, ed. Walter A. Kaufmann and Forrest E. Baird (Englewood Cliffs NJ: Prentice-Hall, 1994) 890-917; esp. 890-95.

[15]As numerous communicators have pointed out, Marx adopts the dialectical scheme from Hegel, but shifts its focus to the material realm. Marx explains the fundamental differences between his use of dialectics and Hegel's in his preface to the second edition of *Capital*: "To Hegel, the life-process of the human brain, i.e., the process of thinking, which, under the name of 'the idea,' he even transforms into an independent subject, is the demiurge of the real world, and the real world is only the external, phenomenal form of 'the Idea.' With me, on the contrary, the ideal is nothing else than the material would reflected by the human mind, and translated into forms of thought" (*Capital* 1:25).

[16]"Dialectic is nothing more than the science of universal laws of motion and evolution in nature, human society and thought." Fredrich Engels, *Herr Eugen Duhrings Revolution in Science*, trans. Emile Burns (New York, 1939) 144; cited by Hook, *From Hegel to Marx*, 75. Although this work was published under Engels's name, it was read to Marx for his approval before publication. In Marxist literature it is commonly cited as *Anti-Duhring*.

[17]Cf. *Capital* 1:391; *Anti-Duhring*, 78.

is the economic realm. The whole movement of history from feudal society to capitalistic society to the time of the proletarian revolution represents an empirically verifiable and irresistible pattern. The dialectic was for Marx not only the clue to historical change, but also a way of thinking. To think dialectically is to think in terms of tension, struggle, conflict, and change; it is to recognize material facts as primary and ideas as secondary, and to know that every epoch is subject to its own laws.[18] For Marx dialectical thought was the highest form of thinking, for it alone enables one to grasp the crucial element in the movement of history.

Marx's anthropology derives from his materialism. Persons are regarded as basically a product of their class. Work determines our associates, interests, standards of living, outlook, and strivings. We are only secondarily molded by family or tied to nation and community; we are what we are because of our place in the class structure. People, of course, are influenced by society, but society in turn has been determined by economic factors. Marx observes: "But the human essence is no abstraction inherent in each single individual. In its reality it is the ensemble of the social relations."[19] Basically Marx was pessimistic about human nature; he finds people generally clinging to tradition, reluctant to change, motivated basically by self-interest, greed, and power. The thirst for power is "the most violent, mean and malignant passion of the human breast, the Furies of private interest."[20] Marx was aware that human beings possess some finer and nobler attributes, of course, but in his thought these are marginal to the human passion for self-interest.[21]

For Marx the goal of history is to establish a new social order. His quarrel with philosophers is pungently put: "The philosophers have only *interpreted* the world, in various ways; the point, however, is to change it."[22] The struggle of the proletariat, therefore, opens up new dimensions

---

[18]*Capital* 1:22-26.

[19]"Theses on Feuerbach," in *Karl Marx and Friedrich Engels: Basic Writings on Politics and Philosophy*, ed. Lewis S. Feuer (Garden City NY: Doubleday/ Anchor Books, 1959) 244.

[20]*Capital* 1:15 (introduction).

[21]See Marx's *Economic and Philosophical Manuscripts*, found in Marx's *Concept of Man*, ed. Erich Fromm (New York: Frederick Unggar, 1966) 131-33.

[22]"Theses on Feuerbach," 245. This quotation is inscribed on Marx's tomb in Highgate Cemetery in London.

of understanding, and educates all those who participate in it. This involvement, not abstract doctrine, is what is crucial for a genuine understanding of the human situation.[23]

It is no wonder that Marx urged the workingmen of the world to unite. The weight of history is with them. The dawn of the new classless society was about to break. The intolerable working conditions and the alienation of men would cease, and no longer would a select minority dominate the lives of the majority. Combining the zeal of the prophet with the certainty of a scientist, Marx felt that he had grasped the essence of history, and he urged humanity to hasten its fulfillment by furthering the revolution of the working classes.

TILLICH'S APPRECIATION OF MARX

Tillich consistently refused to join the ranks of those who dismiss Marx as a diabolical thinker who unleased the wave of communist terror upon the earth. Quite the contrary, he saw many key insights in Marx's thought as having relevance for the twentieth century because Marx interpreted history "in a way which makes even his erroneous prophecies significant."[24] Theologians, Tillich argues, must feel free to appropriate from Marx even as we criticize Marx; the dialogue with Marx must be carried on just as it is with other seminal thinkers both within and without the Christian tradition.[25]

Tillich felt that there are far-reaching analogies between Marx's interpretation of history and the perspective of the Old Testament prophets. Both saw history in dynamic terms, as a struggle between good and evil powers. Humanity is called to identify itself with the historical group that carries on the fight for the good. Redemption is the conquest and extermination of evil in history. In this sense Marx, like the prophets, set

---

[23]Note *Capital* 1:198: "By acting on the external world and changing it, man changes his own nature." See also the extended quotation from Marx's work "Concerning the Production of Consciousness," cited by Hook in *From Hegel to Marx*, 289-90.

[24]"How Much Truth Is There in Karl Marx?" *The Christian Century* 65/36 (3 September 1948): 907.

[25]Tillich, *The Interpretation of History*, trans. N. A. Rasetzki and Elsa L. Talmey (New York: Charles Scribner's Sons, 1936) 66.

himself against the "nonhistorical" interpretations of history which attempt to understand history through categories of nature or space.[26] Tillich felt that Marx retained the sense of radical criticism of society that characterized the prophets, and that this radical criticism has in fact been lost in the established churches.[27] In the name of justice Marx inveighed against nationalism and imperialism; he pointed to a select group upon whom will fall the burden of man's redemption, and felt that there was a necessity to history which made the eventual triumph of the elect group inevitable.[28] Tillich recognized, of course, that Marx had shifted the prophetic concept of transcendence to the material realm of immanence, but he insisted nevertheless that Marx shows a greater affinity to the prophets than do most of the comfortable churches of our day.

With regard to Marx's view of history, Tillich gives priority to Marx's view of *justice*. This is of far greater import than Marx's claim to interpret the historical process scientifically. Both Marx's claim to scientific precision in history and his assertion that the economic factor is the primary force in historical change have been proved wrong.[29] Yet

---

[26]See Tillich's essay, "Historical and Nonhistorical Interpretations of History: A Comparison," in *The Protestant Era* (Chicago: University of Chicago Press, 1957) 16-31.

[27]"Marx and the Prophetic Tradition," *Radical Religion* 1 (Autumn 1935): 21-25.

[28]"Marx and the Prophetic Tradition," 26-29.

[29]Engels himself came to realize that the insistence upon economics as the source of historical change was an oversimplification. In his preface to *Class Struggles in France* (1895), Engels wrote: "When evaluating events or developments of events taken from current history, it is never possible to go all the way back to ultimate economic causes. The materialistic method, only too often, must therefore limit itself to reducing political conflicts, induced by economic development, to conflicts of interest between existing social classes and their factions, and to pointing out that the various political parties represent a more or less adequate political opinion of these same classes or factions. It is obvious that this inevitable neglect of the simultaneous modifications of the economic situation—the very basis of all the events to be studied—can only be a source of error." Cited by Henri Chambre, *From Karl Marx to Mao Tse-Tung* (New York: P. J. Kennedy & Son, 1969) 145. See also Tillich's criticism of Marx on these points in "How Much Truth Is There in Karl Marx?" 906. Reinhold Niebuhr has also criticized Marx on these points in his essay "The

there is an important truth in recognizing the power and significance of the economic factor in life, and in being aware of the concrete physical needs of persons. Marx recognized the existential plight of humanity: dehumanized, alienated, groping for meaning. He recognized that "man is a social being, and his evil as well as his good is dependent on his social existence."[30] Marx was aware that our selfish desires do lead us to exploit our fellow human beings, and he saw the evils inherent in the long working hours, debilitating work, and inadequate wages of nine-teenth-century capitalism. Marx was profoundly aware that amid conditions such as these our very humanity is lost; we become things, tools, objects. Tillich feels that it was this concern for humanity that made Marx a political rebel against the system that fostered these conditions.[31] At any rate, Tillich maintained that Marx's call for justice in the social order was a truly prophetic note, and its relevance remains in the twentieth century.

A third element in Marx's approach to history is likewise noteworthy, namely, that truth (genuine understanding) is a matter of decision and involvement. Marx is in this sense one of the great "existentialist" thinkers. He knew that the person who would know the true meaning of history must be involved in its struggles. Tillich appreciated the fact that Marx not only offered an interpretation of history; he called for a decision and response. Tillich saw in this emphasis a distinct similarity with the *kairos* theme in Christian thought, for both stress that truth lies

---

Anomaly of European Socialism," in *Christian Realism and Political Problems* (New York: Charles Scribner's Sons, 1953) 46-61, and in his discussion of "The Problem of Human Freedom in History," in *Reinhold Niebuhr on Politics*, ed. Harry R. Davis and Robert C. Good (New York: Charles Scribner's Sons, 1960) 45-47.

[30]"Marxism and Christian Socialism," *Christianity and Society* 7/2 (Spring 1942): 14.

[31]"The Person in a Technical Society," in John A. Hutchison, ed., *Christian Faith and Social Action* (New York: Charles Scribner's Sons, 1953) 139-40. Milan Machovec underscored that this humanism is an essential part of Marxism: see his "Marxism and Christianity—A Marxist View," in *Contemporary Religious Issues*, ed. Donald E. Haartsock (Belmont CA: Wadsworth Publishing Co., 1968) 77-79.

beyond the separation of theory and practice, and that truth must be "done" in order to be recognized.[32]

Related to this understanding of truth is Marx's trenchant criticism of the ideologies developed by all societies to justify the status quo. Marx developed this point as a part of his attack on Idealism; as opposed to appeals to a transcendent order, he wanted to stress the primacy of humanity's actual situation. Ideologies that are presented as eternal truths, independent of humanity's concrete situation, distort the actual human situation, and keep us from taking the necessary steps to improve our conditions. This, too, Tillich saw as a valid insight, and he appropriated this into his own understanding of history:

> I owe to Marx, first of all, the insight into the ideological character, not only of idealism but of all systems of thought, religious as well as profane, which as the servants of power hinder, even though unconsciously, the more righteous form of social reality.[33]

Tillich recognized the truth of most of what Marx said about religion as an ideology of the privileged class. The established churches *have* become yoked to the present social order.[34] The needs and yearnings of people other than the middle class go unheeded. Marx can therefore serve as a spur to prod the churches into self-criticism, and to remind the churches that they live by the "Protestant Principle," not by their stake in the established social order.[35]

---

[32]"Marxism and Christian Socialism," 14.

[33]*The Interpretation of History*, 63. See also Tillich's more elaborate discussion of this point in his article "Marx's View of History," 635-36.

[34]"The Attack of Dialectical Materialism on Christianity," *The Student World* 31/3 (third quarter, 1938): 116-17. Tillich cites numerous examples of this: Eastern Orthodoxy, in its Czarist form, and Calvinism in Western Europe both opposed the labor movement; the Vatican strongly sided with the pro-Fascist element in the Spanish Civil War (to say nothing of subsequent concordats with Mussolini and Hitler); the "Austro-Fascism" movement in Austria which violently suppressed the Labor movement; German Lutheran sympathies with National Socialism, etc.

[35]"The Church and Communism," *Religion in Life* 6/3 (Summer 1937): 351-52; cf Tillich's essay, "The Protestant Message and the Man of Today," in *The Protestant Era*, 192-205.

For all these reasons Tillich viewed Marx as a radical prophet, a man with a deep compassion for oppressed people, a powerful interpreter of history, acutely aware of the realities of material needs and political power. In these ways the Christian theologian can learn from Marx, and indeed *must* learn from Marx: "Nobody can understand the character of the present world revolution who was not prepared for it by the Marxian analysis of bourgeois society, its contradictions, and its necessary trends."[36] But Tillich recognized that even as Marx had keen insights, he also made errors of judgment and interpretation, and for these reasons the Christian theologians concerned about the meaning of history must also criticize Marx.

TILLICH'S CRITICISM OF MARX

Tillich feels that Marx erred by being unable to separate the divine from its human, ecclesiastical expressions. Because Marx saw the churches as an extension of the privileged class, he also denied that there was any depth reality to which the churches attempt to bear witness. As a result Marx's interpretation of history is dependent upon immanent processes; it cannot account for the idea of *kairos*, of the external breaking into time, shaking and transforming the temporal.[37] In the last analysis Tillich felt that Marx's perspective on history is one-dimensional: it lacks any awareness of the power of being that sustains all of life and history.

Marx's interpretation of history is furthermore utopian. Since there is no transcendent fulfillment of history possible from Marx's premises, Marx posited his ideal classless society *in* history. This for Tillich is lapsing into the basic error of all utopian schemes: anticipating that in some way human nature and political pressures will be miraculously transformed. Tillich maintains that the establishment of such a society would actually mark a "static vegetative" stage in history, which would not mean the beginning but rather the *end* of history.[38] Basically Tillich felt that "Marx's utopianism derived from his inadequate doctrine of human personhood. Humanity is *not* definable in terms of economic class and fulfillment of human needs; we rather have capacities for creativity

---

[36]"Marxism and Christian Socialism," 18.
[37]"Marxism and Christian Socialism," 15.
[38]*The Interpretation of History*, 188.

as well as selfishness, and deeper needs which changes in our economic status cannot satisfy.[39]

Tillich felt that Marx placed the focal point of history at the wrong place when he pointed to the rise of the proletariat. The future of society cannot be made contingent upon any one class; it will rather rest with the small community of people (which transcends all class lines) who sense the power of "New Being": persons who are aware of the Unconditional, open to the *kairos*, yet aware of the *logos* structure of life and time. In this regard Tillich felt that Marx's vision of history was too narrowly conceived. Tillich appreciated the plight of the working class and recognized its power, but he thought it was fallacious to ascribe to it a messianic destiny.[40]

There are related facets to Marx's thought that Tillich felt may have been relevant for the nineteenth century but which can no longer be substantiated on the basis of twentieth-century knowledge: Marx's theories of work and value, accumulation and concentration of wealth, the scientific study of history, and so forth.[41] Tillich does not take time to refute Marx on these points; he simply says that these facets of Marx's thought were more important for the questions they raised than for the answers Marx gave to them.

It is interesting that Tillich nowhere criticized Marx's doctrine of the necessity of a revolution by the proletariat, although his own identification with the German Social Democratic party suggests his preference for working for social change within the context of existing political structures. The reason for Tillich's silence may lie in his concept of power. He recognized that when a ruling group no longer expresses the will of the majority of citizens, a revolutionary situation is created, and justice in such instances is often on the side of the revolutionary forces. Tillich admits that there are ambiguities involved in determining when the time is ripe for a political revolution, but he was not willing to say that revolutions *ipso facto* are always wrong.[42] "There are situations in which

---

[39]"How Much Truth Is There in Karl Marx?" 907-908.

[40]*The Protestant Era*, 176-77.

[41]"How Much Truth Is There in Karl Marx?" 906.

[42]*The Interpretation of History*, 192-94. For a further assessment of this point, see Theodore Runyon, "Tillich's Understanding of Revolution," in *Theonomy and Autonomy*, ed. John J. Carey (Macon GA: Mercer University

only a revolution (not always a bloody one) can achieve the breakthrough to a new creation."[43] Tillich was not a political revolutionary; on the other hand, for him justice takes priority over pleas for law and order.

MARX AND TILLICH: AN EVALUATION

There is no doubt Karl Marx exerted a greater influence on Tillich than anyone else concerning political consciousness and the interpretation of history. The present analysis, I trust, has helped us understand Tillich's comment that his relationship to Marx was always dialectical, combining a Yes and No.[44] The crucial thing to be noted here is that Tillich always distinguished his evaluation and criticism of Marx from his evaluation of communism. To acknowledge the demonic nature of communism does not therefore imply that Marx should be dismissed as having no value for the Christian understanding history. Tillich recognized that twentieth-century communism has certain affinities with Marx's thought, but he also felt that there are significant distortions of Marx represented in it.[45] This was the fundamental difference between Tillich and Eduard Heimann, one of Tillich's colleagues in the days of the Religious Socialist Movement in Germany in the 1920s. Heimann felt that the totalitarianism of the Soviet Union was the logical consequence of Marx's thought, and therefore claimed that Tillich was unrealistic over the years in trying to reconcile insights from Marx and the Christian faith.[46] The crucial issue is ultimately how Marx is to be interpreted—that is, what aspects of his complex range of thought should be given priority. Tillich, as we have seen, put empahsis on Marx's concern for social justice, dialectical thought, involvement in history, and the need to improve the

---

Press, 1984) 267-80.

[43]*Systematic Theology*, vol. 3 (Chicago: University of Chicago Press, 1963) 344.

[44]"Autobiographical Reflection," in *The Theology of Paul Tillich*, ed. Charles W. Kegley and Robert Walter Bretall (New York: Macmillan, 1952, 1961) 344.

[45]"Autobiographical Reflection.,"

[46]See Heimann's article, "Tillich's Doctrine of Religious Socialism," in Kegley and Bretall, eds., *The Theology of Paul Tillich*, 321-24. It should be noted, however, that this represents a major shift of opinion from Heimann's own writings during the early days of the Religious Socialist Movement in Germany.

material condition of the working class. Tillich refused to see Marx as a dogmatist about either history or politics,[47] and insisted that there is much in Marx that remains valid for our day. It is significant that other theological interpreters today who have made a serious effort to come to grips with Marx have also pointed to Marx's positive contribution to our social and political understanding even as they have criticized various facets of his thought.[48]

Tillich's appreciation of Marx does not mean, of course, that either Marx or Tillich has offered the final word on the interpretation of history, and certainly the topic requires broader treatment than I have been able to provide here. Some significant differences still remain, particularly with regard to any transcendent element in history, and with regard to what group of people have the most influential role in the shaping of history, and whether or not, as liberation theologians claim, God does show a preferential option for the poor.

Tillich's treatment of Marx does suggest, however, that there are some important areas of understanding and action in which Christians and Marxists have much in common as they try to understand the human predicament and work for a better society. It is not surprising that Third World liberation theologians have drawn on Marx's insights in their efforts to bring about a more just society.[49]

---

[47]Engels himself provides evidence that Tillich may be right in this regard. In his "Letters on Historical Materialism," written in the last years of his life, he notes that Marx deplored the rigidity with which some of his followers were interpreting his thought, and repeatedly said, "All I know is that I am not a Marxist." See Feuer, ed., *Karl Marx and Friedrich Engels: Basic Writings on Politics and Philosophy*, 396.

[48]Cf. Roger Shinn, *Christianity and the Problem of History*, 131-39; John Bennett, *Christianity and Communism Today* (New York: Association Press, 1960) 22-57; Alexander Miller, *The Christian Significance of Karl Marx* (New York: Macmillan, 1947) 72-88.

[49]It has been a widely held assumption in Tillich scholarship that after Tillich came to America in 1933 he essentially gave up his Marxian and political interests and turned to the writing of his *Systematic Theology* and other cultural interests. A recent dissertation at the University of Ulster by Bernard Donnelly, "Marxism and the Later Tillich," refutes that assumption and demonstrates that Tillich drew heavily on Marx's thought for all of his career. A monograph based on this dissertation will soon be published by Mercer University Press.

Chapter 3

THEOLOGY AND POLITICS:
INSIGHTS FROM THE GERMAN YEARS

Upon Tillich's death in 1965, the theological world paid homage to him for his many creative endeavors. Systematic theologian par excellence, pioneer in the area of religion and culture, a bridge builder between many different academic disciplines, and a persuasive preacher, Tillich was heralded as one of the few fresh theological voices of the twentieth century and certainly seemed destined to cast a long shadow over theological pursuits for the foreseeable future. It was a strange coincidence of fate that Tillich's demise was followed by a wave of entirely new theological currents: the "secular-city" debate, the "death-of-God" debate, the rapprochement in Protestant-Catholic theology, and the emergence of black theology and political theologies of various stripes. Perhaps the moral here is that theology seldom looks backward in its attempt to speak to ever-changing cultural circumstances; but one apparent consequence of the changing theological scene was that the careful systematic theology of Paul Tillich was frequently shelved as being somehow out of touch with new situations. He seemed to speak to men who saw the world in personal, existentialist categories; his relevance for black people, politically pragmatic people, and revolutionary people was less clear.

This quick waning of interest in Tillich's systematic theology was brought home to me while I was pursuing conversations with Protestant and Roman Catholic scholars in Tübingen, Germany. Amid discussions of the contemporary German theological scene I asked if there were many (or any!) theological groups exploring the implication of Tillich's work. An embarrassed silence followed, and then one theologian noted that there was little interest in Germany in Tillich's ontological approach to theology, and that in fact there was considerable sentiment in Germany that after Tillich came to America and began to develop his systematic theology he removed himself from the matrix and methodologies of Continental theology. The only substantial interest in Tillich's work in modern Germany, I was told, was emerging in the reappraisal of Tillich's early German writings, when Tillich struggled with the issues of history and politics in the days of the Weimar Republic.

Not only in Germany but also in America systematic theology is in trouble, and Tillich's eclipse is undoubtedly due in part to the broader reappraisal of the task and methods of theology that have been forced upon us through a sharpened awareness of historical and cultural contextualism, as well as by the political consciousness that has been so prominent in the theological ethos of the past few years. Yet the same shifts of mood which draw us away from Tillich's ontological categories open up new possibilities for considering the relevance of Tillich's early work. Indeed it is my contention that Tillich's legacy to the twenty-first century may well be in his early writings on politics and history rather than in his later and more formal systematic theology. In America, only James Luther Adams, Ronald Stone, and John Stumme seem to have grasped the significance of Tillich's early work, and we are fortunate that the works they edited and translated have made Tillich's early writings more readily available to the American theological community. I have in mind, of course, Adams's translating and editing of the essays in *The Protestant Era* as well as the many citations in his revised doctoral dissertation, *Paul Tillich's Philosophy of Culture, Science, and Religion*. We have gained further insights into the German period with the publication of *Political Expectation*, also edited by Adams (1971) and J. Mark Thomas's bringing together of various early essays of Tillich's in *The Spiritual Situation in our Technical Society* (1988). In Germany, Gert Hummel and Doris Lax have edited a volume of some of Tillich's very early works (for example, some essays prior to World War I) under the title *Frühe Werke* (Berlin: Walter de Gruyter, 1997, 1998). This has become volume 9 of Tillich's *Gesammelten Werken*. It includes a version of Tillich's *Systematic Theology* dated as early as 1913. But let us now consider the central question: What were the concerns of the early Tillich, and how are they relevant for the theological issues of our day?

I.

Tillich's early writings, covering the quarter-century span from 1912 to 1938, deal with a wide variety of topics, including some of his most suggestive work on the theology of culture, the interaction of theology and philosophy, and the nature of Protestantism. These facets of his work have received a good bit of attention, however, and do not need further amplification here. Rather, I wish to consider two closely related yet distinct aspects of Tillich's early work: his writings on politics and history. Tillich's insights in both these areas are germane to our present theological interests, inasmuch as the ramifications of liberation theology and of the meaning of history are very much with us.

To appreciate Tillich's approach to, and involvement with, the political situation of Germany in the 1920s and 1930s we need to recall some of the particular problems of that epoch: the emergence of the socialist parties as a challenge to the old structures and institutions of German life; the growing strength of the National Socialist (Nazi) Party; the opposition of the Lutheran Church to the parties of the left; the polarization of German society into parties of the left and right; the concern of a small group of German theologians and intellectuals to find a *via media* between the left and right. Tillich's own political stance—of helping to found and work for the Religious Socialist movement, is well known, and it is not my intent here to retell that story.[1] It is important, however, to note how Tillich appraised the strengths and weaknesses of the theological left and right, and how he assessed both in light of the Christian claim.

In an early article Tillich argued that conservative and liberal political thought are rooted in different facets of human experience. Every man senses his own affinity with the creative ground of life; we are born into a stream of history; we are yoked by blood and memory to forebears. There is a mysterious "whence" that impinges upon our consciousness, and it is our dependence upon that mysterious origin that Tillich maintains is "the foundation of every conservative and romantic thought in politics."[2] The themes of political conservatism—law, order, structure,

---

[1]See Tillich's introduction to *The Protestant Era* (Chicago: University of Chicago Press, 1957) xiii-xvii; and Eduard Heimann, "Tillich's Doctrine of Religious Socialism," in *The Theology of Paul Tillich*, ed. Charles W. Kegley and Robert W. Bretall (New York: Macmillan, 1964) 312-25. The most thorough study of the Religious Socialist Movement is that of Eberhard Amelung, "Religious Socialism as an Ideology: A Study of the 'Kairos Circle' in Germany, 1919–1933" (Th.D. diss., Harvard University, 1962).

[2]"The Two Roots of Political Thinking," in *The Interpretation of History*, trans. N. A. Rasetzki and Elsa L. Talmey (New York: Scribner's, 1936) 207.

authority, continuity—are seen thereby not just as an ideology of recalcitrance but as legitimate extensions of a theological awareness of human nature. Liberal political thought, by contrast, derives from the related experience of coming to know change; the "is" of personal and social life is confronted by the "ought," or, as Tillich says, the myth of our origin is finally broken by an unconditioned demand.[3] The themes of liberal, democratic, and socialistic politics-justice, equality, freedom, change-are extensions of the human realization that there is a call for newness which breaks into the security of established social structures. Pivotal for Tillich in this appraisal is his conclusion that the demand for change takes priority over the desire to preserve the familiar; the dynamic supersedes the static. Tillich allied himself with the political left because he felt that whatever its weaknesses, it was more clearly the political response of those who wanted justice in the social order.

The political left, however, covered a broad spectrum in the Weimar Republic, just as it does in contemporary America. Tillich repeatedly analyzed and criticized the political positions of the Communists and Socialists even as he sought to show their strengths. Concerning communism, Tillich opposed all the tendencies of political and ecclesiastical conservatives to depict communism as solely a means of Bolshevik terrorism. Against the social and political entrenchment of the German Lutheran Church, Tillich insisted that the message of communism was essentially a secularized and politicized form of Christian prophecy. The basic call of communism is for social justice; it is open toward the future with a revolutionary eschatology. Furthermore, the communist challenge to both capitalism and nationalism exposes the demonic elements in those ideologies. The political stance of the Marxists has to be opposed insofar as it operates totally within a secular realm and incorporates lies and tyranny to attain its goals; but Tillich, clearly disillusioned with the conservatism of the established churches, argued that they should get their own houses in order before condemning the Marxists.[4]

---

[3]"The Two Roots of Political Thinking," 208.

[4]Tillich *always* distinguished between communism as developed in Russia and the social and political analyses of Karl Marx. Although he did not feel that Russian communism represented a valid extension of Marx's thought, he acknowledged that various European Communist parties retained a prophetic truth against capitalistic societies. See Tillich's articles "Der Socialismus als

The Socialists, considerably stronger politically than the Communists, posed other problems for Tillich. Tillich wrote extensively during the 1920s and early 1930s concerning the strengths and weaknesses of socialism. On the positive side, he felt that socialism was "the greatest and most effective of the movements in opposition to capitalist society."[5] It correctly grasped that harmonious order will not come to any society through the competitive process of free economic powers, and as a party it was prepared to take the necessary steps to establish a sound, balanced economy. It therefore had a specific goal and could offer hope to the working class. In a politically prophetic way, socialism bears witness to the human situation, its distortion and its promise. Negatively, however, socialist ideology does not allow for the spiritual dimension of life which can break through historical circumstances and make all things new (it was, in other words, too secular for Tillich); it furthermore incorporated elements of utopianism. Tillich and his counterparts (the most notable of whom, for American purposes, was Eduard Heimann) consequently identified themselves as *Religious* Socialists and carried on a "lovers" quarrel with the Social Democratic Party. Tillich wrote:

> It is the task of Religious Socialism to carry through a radical criticism of socialism, but on the ground of socialism itself. Its criticism must not weaken the passion of the proletarian struggle. Rather it must strengthen this passion in that it deepens it; in that it holds up to socialism what the true meaning of its movement is, and makes this meaning the critical standard of the actual facts.[6]

If Tillich was dialectical in his relationship to the political left, he was uncompromising in his opposition to the political right. The right rested upon and sought to perpetuate the capitalistic economy, which, in Tillich's opinion, had already wrought much evil in Western societies. In

---

Kirchenfrage" (1919), *Gesammelte Werke*, vol. 2 (Stuttgart: Evangelisches Verlagswerk, 1962) 13-20, and "The Church and Communism," *Religion in Life* 6 (Summer 1937): 347-57.

[5]*The Religious Situation* (New York: Henry Holt, 1932) 111-12. This work was originally published in 1925 as *Die Religiöse Lage der Gegenwart*.

[6]*Religiöse Verwirklichung* (Berlin: Furche, 1930) 208. A number of the essays (but not all) in the original German volume were translated by James Luther Adams and included in *The Protestant Era*.

its appeal to unify Germany around a supernationalism it carried with it the demonic capacity to destroy nuances of judgment, justice, and diplomacy. Most crucially, however, politics of the right loses the capacity to distinguish the distance between God and the present political situation. Tillich in fact broke with his former colleague Emanuel Hirsch on this very point, when Hirsch endorsed the Nazi movement and its call for a "New Germany."[7] The political right, just like the left, is prone to a utopianism that overlooks the ambiguities of human history. The fact is, Tillich argued, that the politics of the right leads finally to the idea of a totalitarian state—a state in which culture, art, science, and social life are regulated, personal freedom is curtailed, minorities are persecuted, and even religious liberties are restricted. Born in insecurity and appealing for "reintegration" of a people, a totalitarian state destroys even as it ostensibly builds. Law and order are achieved at the expense of justice, and this for Tillich repudiates the prophetic element in the Christian tradition.[8]

The *via media* advocated by Tillich between the politics of the left and that of the right was unsuccessful, primarily because Religious Socialism remained an intellectual movement and never got the support of workers or middle-class churchmen. Many of its goals and ideals were, however, eventually absorbed into the consciousness of post-World War II Germany. Our task here, however, is not simply to review Tillich's early political thought but rather to suggest what there is in his political theology that can shed some light on our present quandaries.

In his later reflections upon his early political writings, Tillich acknowledged that he had perhaps been too romantic in thinking that German society would respond to its *kairos* moment along the lines of a religiously informed socialism; and in fairness we must note that in his later life Tillich was more cautions about advocating specific political strategies. Caution furthermore dictates that we acknowledge the major differences in time, culture, and political contexts between Germany in the 1920s and 1930s and America in later decades. Much of what Tillich

---

[7]This whole episode has been summarized by David Hopper in *Tillich: A Theological Portrait* (Philadelphia: Lippincott, 1968) 65-100.

[8]Tillich's fullest exposition about the politics of the right is in "The Totalitarian State and the Claims of the Church," *Social Research* 1 (November 1934): 405-33.

wrote at that time is dated and of interest only to historians. Yet at least three of Tillich's insights into the theology of politics are still germane to our situation. We too find ourselves in a polarized society; we are trying to cope with the breakdown of old mythologies and we now hear appeals for violent and/or nonviolent revolution. Our political conscious-ness was heightened by, for example, the Vietnam War, and sharp criticisms have been leveled by the youth culture which generally rejects both the parties and policies of traditional American politics.

II.

Tillich's work cautions us, first of all, to beware of the utopianism of the left. The initial appeal of the left for social justice is bound to be compelling for those whose worldview is in any way shaped by the prophetic tradition, but one must be cautious about any naïve approach to history that assumes that the ideal society can actually be established. Both an anthropological realism and a dialectical understanding of history remind us that all movements for social reform create new ambiguities and antitheses. Political approaches to justice can only be approximate, and a crusade mentality distorts both vision and honesty. Tillich insisted that the truth in the political left's call for justice has to be known "existentially," that is, through involvement, but even amid activity one has to retain the capacity to think realistically and dialectically.

Tillich reminds us secondly to be cautious of the totalitarianism of the left as well as the right. Secular political ideologies of both extremes can deny the basic elements of human dignity and refuse to acknowledge alternate viewpoints on political priorities. The left as well as the right can settle for trite slogans and epithets to avoid analysis and criticism; both contain embers which, when fanned, can flame into totalitarianism. It is the religious dimension to political thought which insists upon a humanism as a *sine qua non* of political integrity. Coalition politics is not only pragmatically expedient but also humanistically helpful, insofar as it broadens the base of power and keeps any one group from operating dogmatically. Political power, in Tillich's perspective, does not rest ultimately upon the threat of force (as theorists of both the left and right maintain), but in fact has a higher expression in a government's *restraint,* or even willingness to renounce control.[9] The secret of political power, argued Tillich, is not in coercion but in "inner might," in the respect for human dignity and the continued search for justice. Among recent American theologians of politics, perhaps Peter Berger stands closest to Tillich's orientation on this point.[10]

A third point at which Tillich has relevance for our political situation is in his serious grappling with Marxism. Tillich had a lifelong interest in Marx, whom he unashamedly called one of the great prophets of the nineteenth century. In one sense Tillich was the embodiment of a Christian-Marxist dialogue long before this became fashionable in theological circles.[11] As we noted in chapter 2, Tillich derived from Marx his themes of social justice, the destructive capacities of capitalistic-industrial states, and the ideologies which are developed by ruling groups to justify their place in the status quo. In an early article Tillich wrote: "I owe to Marx, first of all, the insight into the ideological character, not only of idealism but of all systems of thought, religious as well as profane, which as the servants of power hinder, even though unconsciously, the more righteous form of social reality."[12] Not only does this insight remind us to keep a critical distance from the mythologies of America's political parties, but it also can serve as a spur to realize that which lies at the heart of leftist criticisms of the American social order. Whether the New Left in America is dead or merely dormant, there are few of us who would not admit the trenchant relevance for the American situation of analyses such as the so-called "Port Huron Statement."[13]

---

[9]See Tillich's essay, "The Problem of Power," in *The Interpretation of History*, esp. 198-202.

[10]See Berger's "Between System and Horde," in Peter L. Berger and Richard John Neuhaus, *Movement and Revolution* (New York: Doubleday/Anchor Books, 1970) esp. 13-30.

[11]For elaboration of this point, see chap. 2.

[12]*The Interpretation of History*, 63.

[13][Editor's note.] The Port Huron Statement was the founding document of the 1960s protest group, Students for a Democratic Society. The document was drafted by Tom Hayden, a cofounder of SDS, and adopted at the meeting of sixty founding members of SDS at Port Huron, Michigan, 11-15 June 1962. The statement voices concerns that, ostensibly, a majority of the people of the U.S. choose to ignore global problems such as revolution, overpopulation, poverty,

Tillich did not, of course, appropriate Marx uncritically, and on a number of points he criticized the arguments of both Marx and his followers. In areas where Marx has been shown to be wrong (that is, his theories of work and value, accumulation and concentration of wealth, the scientific study of history, and so forth) Tillich simply said that these facets of Marx's thought were more important for the questions they raised than for the answers Marx gave to them. It is interesting to note (amid our current waves of "theologies of revolution") that Tillich nowhere criticized Marx's doctrine of the necessity of a revolution by the proletariat, even though his own identification with the socialists indicated his preference for working for social change within the context of existing political structures. The reason for Tillich's silence may lie in his concept of power. He recognized that when a ruling group no longer expresses the will of a majority of citizens, a revolutionary situation is created, and justice in such instances is often on the side of the revolutionaries. Tillich admitted that there are ambiguities involved in determining when the time is ripe for a political revolution, but he was not willing to say that revolutions *ipso facto* are always wrong.[14]

To contemporary political analysts who see the future evolving "without Marx or Jesus,"[15] Tillich's answer would be clear: try *both* Marx *and* Jesus. There is much in Marx that prepares us for the understanding of man in social and economic categories, and in Tillich's perspective no viable political theology can ignore these emphases.

There are, of course, limitations on the value of Tillich's political analyses of his German years, perhaps most notably centering around the place he assigned to capitalism as the major destructive and disintegrating force of the twentieth century.[16] Yet in his assessment of heated issues

---

and war. Hayden and the SDS believed such issues would become America's if left unresolved (they were already America's problems). So SDS counseled for direct action and involvement in making history, rather than merely dwelling on what is past.

[14]*The Interpretation of History*, 192-94.

[15][Editor's note.] See, e.g., Jean François Revel, *Without Marx or Jesus: The New American Revolution Has Begun*, trans. J. F. Bernard, with an afterword by Mary McCarthy (London: MacGibbon & Kee, 1970; Garden City NY: Doubleday, 1971).

[16]Tillich's appraisal of capitalism has been criticized by Clark A. Kucheman

and polarized political opinion, particularly in his calls for realism, humanism, and demythologizing of ideologies, Tillich still has a relevant word for our generation.

III.

There is a second area in which the early Tillich has relevance for our time, and that is in his writings on the meaning of history. It is possible, of course, to see the problems of history as a perennial problem for theology: the twentieth century has seen the problem raised by Harnack, repudiated by Barth, redefined by Bultmann, and reintroduced by Pannenberg. It lies beyond the scope of this article to trace this interesting and complex debate in detail; suffice it to say that the work of Pannenberg, so influential in German theology, has to be seen as a reaction to the Bultmannian existentialist approach to history. Pannenberg has denied the distinctions the Bultmannians make between *Historie* and *Geschichte* and the subsequent redefinition by Bultmann as to what "historical existence" means. Pannenberg has wanted to yoke modern theology more closely to historical and exegetical modes of biblical inquiry, and to set the stage for a theological historiography that would provide a historical argument for the factuality of the resurrection. Most recent evaluations of the problem of history have centered around the strengths and weaknesses of Pannenberg's endeavors.[17]

To consider Tillich's early writings on history gives us some major alternatives to Pannenberg's work. Although there are complex facets to Tillich's approach to history which are beyond what we can consider here, it is important to note that Tillich always opposed the historical positivists who wanted to base Christianity upon scholarly evaluation of past events. History, argued Tillich in his early writings, "is the totality of remembered events, which are determined by free human activity and

---

in his article "Professor Tillich: Justice and the Economic Order," *The Journal of Religion* (January, 1966): 165-83. Kucheman feels that capitalistic economics have shown more flexibility than Tillich thought was possible, and that it is not self-evident that the social ownership of the principal means of production will rectify the problems of advanced industrial societies.

[17]See, e.g., the volume edited by James M. Robinson and John B. Cobb, Jr., *Theology as History* (New York: Harper & Row, 1967).

are important for the life of human group."[18] History involves free choices as to what is meaningful; it is filled with decisions and risks, of the *kairos* breaking in on the *logos*. The clue to history is not in proving past events but rather in purposeful action in the present. He wrote:

> The meaning of history can be discerned only in meaningful historical activity. The key to history is historical action, not a point above history; historical activity is active participation in the life of a historical group. The meaning of history manifests itself in the self-understanding of a historical group.[19]

Tillich, in other words, is not interested as much in historical *knowledge* as he is in historical *consciousness*: the awareness of one's ultimate fate in history, and of being so penetrated by the forces of history as to discern the creative significance of the present moment. For Tillich, he who would understand history must be an actor within the context of events rather than a spectator:

> Since the only entrance to the interpretation of history is historical action, there is no serious grappling with the problem of history which has not been born out of the necessity for coming to a present historical decision.[20]

As a political theologian, then, Tillich attempted to yoke together political action with an understanding of history. His legacy to our generation in this regard is to remind us that from a Christian standpoint the problem of history always has contemporary implications. The historical question is not just "What can we learn about the past?" It also implies "What does the present require?" To follow Tillich's reasoning here opens up a new range of questions about history as a problem in contemporary theology.

---

[18]"The Kingdom of God and History," in H. G. Wood, ed., *The Kingdom of God and History* (London: Allen & Unwin, 1938) 108. This article was prepared by Tillich for the Oxford Conference on Church, Community, and State in 1937.

[19]Cited by James Luther Adams, "Tillich's Interpretation of History," in Kegley and Bretall, eds., *The Theology of Paul Tillich*, 295.

[20]"The Kingdom of God and History," 106.

IV.

A friend remarked to me several years ago that the impressive thing about Albert Schweitzer was that whereas many people talked about Africa, Schweitzer *went*. Similarly we can say that the impressive thing about the early Tillich as a political theologian was that he not only theorized about historical events, he was also deeply involved. The Berlin Circle of Religious Socialists, church conferences, youth meetings, anti-Nazi activities, helping the Jews—Tillich was there. Perhaps Tillich would feel that he did not live and write in vain if either by word or action he inspired a later generation of Christians to become serious participants in the ongoing struggle for justice in the arena of politics.

Chapter 4

TILLICH AS BIBLICAL INTERPRETER

Anyone who wishes to pursue Tillich's foundations and assumptions has to deal with his approach to the Bible and to biblical authority. As we pointed out in chapter 1, from childhood on, nourished by the home of a pastor of the Evangelical Church (predominantly Lutheran), Tillich was exposed to the Bible as a sourcebook for Christian life and faith. His educational pilgrimage, however, brought him to a different sense of the Bible, and he subsequently separated himself from biblical literalists, archaeologists, conservative theologies, and technical historical-critical interpreters. His view of the Bible and its authority was one reason why conservative Christians on both sides of the Atlantic viewed him as a "dangerous" theologian.[1]

Tillich's understanding of the meaning and significance of the Bible is rooted in his orientation as a philosophical theologian. He was interested in how the claims and language of philosophy (for example, "The Ultimate," "The One," "Being") relate to the testimony of the Bible about God as Creator, Sustainer, and Redeemer. He was basically more interested in ontology than in technical biblical scholarship. He felt that theological language emerges because people have "a special encounter

---

[1]Tillich's works which bear on this topic include "The Problem of Theological Method," in *The Journal of Religion* 27/1 (January 1947); this is reprinted in various anthologies. See also *Systematic Theology*, vol. 1 (1951); *Biblical Religion and the Search for Ultimate Reality*, the James W. Richard Lectures in the Christian Religion, University of Virginia 1951–1952 (Chicago: University of Chicago Press, 1955) and *Dynamics of Faith* (Harper & Row, 1957) esp. chap. 3 on "Symbols of Faith." Relevant secondary literature includes Reinhold Niebuhr's essay "Biblical Thought and Ontological Speculation in Tillich's Theology," in *The Theology of Paul Tillich*, 2nd ed., ed. Charles W. Keglely (New York: Pilgrim Press, 1982) 252-65; O. G. A. Calvert, "Paul Tillich and Biblical Theology," *The Scottish Journal of Theology* 29/1 (1976): 27-48; and Bob Price, "Homilectical Hermeneutics in Paul Tillich," *The Drew Gateway* 50/1 (1979): 15-24.

with reality" which enables them to become ultimately concerned about
that reality. As a "boundary thinker" (as he liked to call himself) he
viewed his special task as speaking to these who stand on the boundaries
(or outside) of the community of faith. He described his work as
"apologetic" theology, and addressed much of his writing to these who
wondered if the Bible has *any* significance in a secularized and techno-
logical age.

Tillich viewed the Bible as a confessional document of the Christian
community. Although he respected the integrity of Judaism, he felt that
Christians could legitimately read the Old Testament in the light of how
it prepared early Christians to understand and respond to Jesus as the
Christ. The history, language, rites, and ideas of Israel are important
insofar as they created the atmosphere in which the "new reality" of Jesus
was received and interpreted. The New Testament, on the other hand, is
important because it depicts how Jesus was perceived and received as the
Christ. Every New Testament writer was in some way a witness to the
Christ event. The critical feature of the Christ event is that it gives us a
decisive manifestation of the Ground of Being (Tillich's favorite term for
the Holy). Jesus is the "New Being," in whom humanity finds reunion,
reconciliation, and restoration. The Bible is the primary source that helps
us understand the meaning of New Being. The concept of New Being can
therefore be said to be Tillich's hermeneutical principle.

The Bible is not, however, the only source which Christians need to
utilize. Church history and the insights of the history of religion and
culture are also necessary to clarify the nature of the Power of Being. But
the Bible can be said to be the *basic* source for Christian life and belief
because it contains the original documents about the events on which the
Christian church is founded. It witnesses to that of which it is a part. It
tells a story; it describes a saving reality, and it invites readers to receive
and know that reality.

Tillich rejected all literal interpretations of the Bible, and also the
exalted sense of the Bible as "the Word of God" as championed by Karl
Barth. (In their lifetimes Tillich and Barth were commonly used by other
theologians and teachers as polar opposites of how to interpret the Bible
and "do" theology.) Tillich felt that modern interpreters need to utilize the
historical-critical method, but also to show "devotional-interpretive"
sensitivity since the Bible deals with matters of ultimate concern. "Only
such free historical work," he wrote, "united with the attitude of ultimate

concern, can open the Bible to the systematic theologian as his basic source" (*Systematic Theology* 1:36).

The Bible, then, is not important for its historical names, dates, battles, ceremonies, liturgical materials, apocalyptic visions, or wisdom documents. Historical inaccuracies or omissions do not negate its authority. It has significance because it points to a saving reality that has appeared in history to manifest a new way of being. Biblical language is symbolic, and has power because symbols participate in that to which they point.

Tillich did not believe in any "pure" interpretation of a biblical text. He knew that all interpreters are influenced by their own times, denominational histories, and by what previous exegets have done. It is impossible to leap across two thousand years and neatly transpose biblical terminology and ideas into this new age. Knowledge of the contents of the Bible *per se* has no salvific knowledge either. The clue to understanding the Bible, and the truth of the Christian proclamation, is to experience the reality of "New Being" in our own lives. Tillich has been called the most experience-orientated Protestant theologian since Schleiermacher.

Tillich's experiential and meditative hermeneutic enabled him to preach powerfully from biblical texts. His three books of sermons—*The Shaking of the Foundations* (1953), *The New Being* (1955), and *The Eternal Now* (1963)—are still in print and are regarded by Tillich scholars as some of his finest work.[2]

---

[2]For a detailed consideration of Tillich as a preacher, see William Terrell Sanders, "Paul Tillich: Apologetic Preacher of the Christian Faith" (Ph.D. diss., Florida State University, 1983) esp. chaps. 3, 4, and 5.

Chapter 5

TILLICH'S *THE COURAGE TO BE* AFTER FIFTY YEARS

In the fall semester of 1950, Paul Tillich delivered the Terry Lectures at Yale on the topic "The Courage to Be." The Terry Lectures are stipulated to be "lectures on religion in the light of science and philosophy," and the lecturer has traditionally been invited by an interdisciplinary university committee made up of representatives from the Divinity School, the Department of Philosophy, and the natural sciences. Tillich's lectures were the twenty-seventh in the series, surely one of the most distinguished lecture series in the United States. Tillich delivered four lectures, which became the basis for chapters 1, 4, 5, and 6 in the published version. Between the lectures and their publication, he added chapter 2 on "Being, Nonbeing, and Anxiety" and chapter 3 on "Pathological Anxiety, Vitality, and Courage," and expanded some of the material in the original lectures. A copy of the original lectures is found in the Paul Tillich Archives at Harvard.

The book, *The Courage to Be*, was published in November 1952.[1] It quickly moved into a second printing in January 1953 and a third printing in February 1953. The book has become one of the all-time best-sellers for Yale University Press. As long ago as December 1991, an official of the Press told me that the book (still in print) has sold more than 35,000 copies in hardback and more than 411,000 (!) copies in paperback. Although virtually all of Tillich's books would be considered best-sellers by their various publishers, *The Courage to Be* is in a class by itself. Its continuing sales attest to its popularity as a text in college and seminary

---

[1] *The Courage to Be*, Based on the Terry Lectures delivered at Yale University (New Haven CT: Yale University Press, 1952; first perfectbound [paperback] edition, 1959); 2nd ed.: with an introduction by Peter J. Gomes, Yale Note Bene series (New Haven CT: Yale University Press, 2000). The second edition was published as a book/text, computer file, and online as a netLibrary eBook.

courses and to the fact that two different generations continue to find it a relevant and powerful book. It is appropriate, therefore, that fifty years after its publication, we pause and look back at this remarkable volume.

Before we comment on the book from today's perspective, however, it is important to note the historical political context in which Tillich wrote the book. World War II had been over only five years when Tillich first delivered his lectures. The Berlin Wall went up in 1948 and was answered by the famous Berlin airlift. The Korean War broke out in the summer of 1950. Harry Truman was president of the U.S. The Cold War and its ideology had a major influence on American cultural and political thinking. The McCarthy era was fomenting suspicion of any liberal political thinking. In his "Reply to Interpretation and Criticism" in the Kegley-Bretall volume *The Theology of Paul Tillich*, Tillich characterized this as a time of "void" and of waiting; it was not a time of kairos and revelation. Tillich clearly thought that in that *Zeitgeist* existentialism captured the mood and offered a viable alternative to despair and to popular religion. There can be no understanding of the analysis or prescriptions of this book, however, is one does not acknowledge the cultural and political climate of that period.

In this chapter I shall concentrate on some of the distinctive themes of *The Courage to Be*, and then raise some questions about its significance for today's intellectual and theological climate.

I.

1. The first thing to say is that this volume is vintage Tillich as a philosophical theologian. Tillich conveyed those interests in volume 1 of his *Systematic Theology*, in *Love, Power, and Justice*, and in his *Biblical Religion and the Search for Ultimate Reality*, but *The Courage to Be* is the richest example of his work on the boundaries of philosophy and theology. It shows how Tillich weaves together issues from the Western philosophical tradition with broader Christian interests of self-affirmation, wholeness, and salvation. His thinking in this book follows the lines and language of Athens more than it does of Jerusalem. His treatment of courage as an ontological category rather than a virtue or ethical act was a bold and creative contribution to Christian theology. In chapter 1 Tillich traces the concept of courage ("the essential self-affirmation of one's being"—what Plato saw as bridging the cleavage between reason and desire) from Plato and Aristotle through the Stoics, Aquinas, Spinoza, and

Nietzsche. He calls Nietzsche "the most impressive and effective representative of what could be called a 'philosophy of life' (p. 27) and praises Nietzsche for developing a philosophy of courage in opposition to the decadence which characterized his generation. In Western Christian thought, Nietzsche is commonly dismissed as a genius gone mad, and as an opponent to the Judeo-Christian ethic, and/or as the one whose interest in the superman (*Übermensch*) laid the foundation for Nazi ideology. Inspired by Tillich's analysis, I bought Heidegger's four volumes on Nietzsche and have begun a fresh appraisal of Nietzsche's constructive work. That reading has stretched and lubricated some of my hardened categories.

2. *The courage to Be* is based on Tillich's distinctive reading of the history of Western thought into two streams: (1) the rationalist, idealistic, and classical stream; and (2) the "philosophers of life," who deal with conflict, despair, and brokenness in the human condition. This analysis of two major streams in Western thought is later repeated by Tillich in his *Systematic Theology* (see 1:9-11 and 265-66) as well as in his *A History of Christian Thought*.[2] In this typology Tillich clearly sides with the philosophers of life (Jakob Böhme, Schelling, Schopenhauer, Feuerbach, Marx, Nietzsche, Dilthey, Bergson, Simmel, William James, Berdyaev, Heidegger) "who give us a more accurate understanding of the brokenness, anxiety, and despair which characterize the life of modern people." His typology may be debatable but is critical for his analysis: it lays the groundwork for his embracing of existentialism.

3. One is struck in rereading this volume how much it depends on existentialism as a philosophical viewpoint that correctly assesses the modern situation. In 1950–1952 Tillich was persuaded that modern women and men were living in a meaningless world, and that they had lost any notice of selfhood that derives from a spiritual center. This lostness, of course, creates despair, and the issue for Tillich was how we can come to a "courage of despair" which can take us beyond meaning-lessness.

We should note in passing that this reading of the human situation at that time was expressed most persuasively by American intellectuals in

---

[2]The most recent edition *A History of Christian Thought* (2nd rev. ed.) was edited by Carl E. Braaten (New York: Harper & Row, 1968).

the Northeast, many of whom had European roots. The residual impact
of World War II remained with them, and American culture seemed to
them to offer only materialism, naiveté, and folk religion. There appeared
to be no answers to the anxieties about death, meaninglessness, and
condemnation. Existentialism alone seemed to provide an honest analysis
of the depth of our pains, and give us "the courage to face things as they
are, and to express the anxiety of meaninglessness" (p. 43).

Against this dour and depressing analysis, we should also remember
that 1952 was also the year Dwight Eisenhower was elected president of
the United States, when millions of people affirmed "I like Ike"; when
the great boom in Protestant churches was beginning to emerge; and
when prosperity began to spread through the American middle class. This
raises the implicit question of just who Tillich was describing in his 1952
analysis that "modern man has lost all meaning." Perhaps his famous
analysis said more about Tillich and his melancholy friends than about
life in general. Tillich spoke to and for a certain type of person, but we
can recognize today that analysis of the "human condition" is a more
complex task than Tillich thought.

4. The major theological theme that Tillich finally comes to in the
book, of course, is that modern persons need to find the "God beyond
God," that is, to go "beyond the God of theism." This point electrified
Tillich's listeners in 1950 and caused heated discussions in the Divinity
School and Philosophy Department. Was Tillich leaving Christianity
behind? Is the world now post-Christian? Tillich argued that being
grasped by this Power will transcend the human tendencies to lose
ourselves in the identity of large masses or to be driven to despair in our
own individual forsakenness. Tillich's version was a bold and suggestive
idea. It was not put before the broad Christian public, however, until John
A. T. Robinson popularized it in his best-selling *Honest to God* in 1963.
Tillich's concept still lays bare the shallowness of popular religion and
the uncritical theism of mainline churches, and invites us to fresh
theological thinking on the "God-issue."

5. It is also worth noting that, in this analysis of the human plight and
of our need to "accept our acceptance" by the "God above God," only
twice in 190 pages does Tillich even make passing references to Jesus.
It is as though this entire essay were an attempt to analyze the human
situation and to point to a solution through the constructs of philosophy
rather than the categories of biblical faith. That is one of the things so

puzzling about the book to me when I first read it in 1954 and which still make it problematic to conservative Christian readers. The book stands in tension with Tillich's later writings about the "New Being," and fuels the criticism that Jesus is not really necessary for Tillich's theological system. At its best, the book is a model of how Christian themes can be recast into an alternative language scheme. It raises important theological and philosophical issues about truth and language. What, in the last analysis, is the truth we are trying to describe in Christian theological discourse?

6. On a critical note, we must acknowledge that Tillich's ontological language and tendency to utilize categories such as the "threat of nonbeing" make this book difficult reading. Phrases like "the threat against man's ontic self-affirmation" are not on everyone's lips these days. It is further true that Tillich's analysis of the human predicament does not distinguish between male and female, black and white, majority and minority, or rich and poor. He felt that there was a universality to the human plight that transcended all such categories. Both the language of the book and the assumptions underlying it seem dated—but, then, that is generally the case with books that are fifty years old.

II.

The critiical question for us today is whether we think Tillich's analysis of the human situation is still accurate. Is it, for example, an analysis which is helpful to women? Is it an analysis that is illuminating for persons of color, or for persons in Third World contexts? The answer is ambiguous, primarily because of Tillich's language. We know that today many segments of the human population are still struggling for identity, dignity, a decent level of life, and for political rights. Maybe all of these struggles express diverse ways that people are seeking "the courage to be." I think we have to recognize that many component parts of the world's population (including those of Judeo-Christian ranks) are seeking an answer as to where and how to find "the courage to be." Woman might find it in the bonds of sisterhood, as Mary Daly has suggested. Black persons might find it in the struggle to overcome racism and in building up the bonds of the black community, as James Cone has suggested. Latin Americans and other dispossessed people might find it in a struggle for justice and political identity, as Gustavo Gutierrez and other liberation theologians have suggested. Soviet citizens and Eastern

Europeans might find it in the struggle for a new society and new economic structures. White middle class persons might find it in quests for personal spirituality and commitments to causes that will help us build a better society and a better world, for example, in the peace movement, the environmental movement, or in the struggles against racism, sexism, and classism. With the end of the Cold War and the de-escalation of the arms race, we probably would find fewer contemporary persons identifying with Tillich's philosophical analysis of the human situation and the type of solution he offers.

Yet we must be cautious before dismissing Tillich's analysis of fifty years ago. There are still pockets of despair in America amid the circles of poverty, drug abuse, and homelessness. Many young people today are frozen out of professional employment. AIDS victims know fear and despair, as do virtually all people in racial ghettos. People who bear pain and disappointment know the depths that Tillich describes even if they would not express it in his language. To reread *The Courage to Be* today is to be reminded that brokenness still pervades the human condition, and that people still need some words of hope.

On another note, Tillich reminds us of the ongoing relevance of existentialism as a theological perspective. Feminist scholars have been noting how the themes of existentialism have relevance for feminist theological work. Wanda Berry of Colgate University read an impressive paper on this theme at the 1991 meeting of the American Academy of Religion in Kansas City. At a time when most American theologians have been willing to regard existentialism as a post-World War II theological fad, Berry and other feminists remind us of its passion for meaning, its intensity, its recognition of the irrational forces in life, and its ability to press into the deeper depths of human experience. That is a formidable legacy, and suggests that there is still much in that way of thinking that needs to be preserved in a postmodern world.

Several Tillich scholars have asked how historical thinking or historical consciousness influences *The Courage to Be*. The book is an essay in philosophical theology and as such does not directly engage questions of history. Tillich broadly treats the history of Western thought about courage through Plato, Aristotle, the Stoics, Thomas Aquinas, Spinoza, and Nietzsche. In *The Courage to Be*, Tillich implicitly adopts an existentialist interpretation of history that is very close to Bultmann's, namely, that the meaning of history is not in its pastness, nor in sagas, stories, or remembered events. The meaning of history lies in our present situation, in choices we make, and in creatively grasping our present existence. As suggestive as these insights are, this in not one of Tillich's primary texts on the understanding of history.

In sum, I think *The Courage to Be* was, and is, a brilliant book. If Tillich had written nothing else in the field of philosophical theology, this book would give him a special niche in that discipline. In a time when creative scholars are searching for new models of theological discourse and fresh language systems, Tillich's work is still suggestive and exemplary. This is not the easiest book of Tillich's to read, and it is not an ideal book with which to begin the study of Tillich.

For what it is, however, as an expression of the theme of the Terry lectures—"religion in the light of science and philosophy"—it is a classic work. If from today's perspective we can see terminology in it which is unfamiliar, I would still say of Tillich what he once said of Marx: that the questions he asked are so important that it does not matter if his terminology needs revising.

Chapter 6

A RESPONSE TO ALEXANDER C. IRWIN'S *EROS TOWARD THE WORLD*[1]

The space constraints of this collection of essays keep me from saying all I would like to say about this interesting and remarkable book by Alexander Irwin. For clarity my remarks are organized in three categories: (1) reflections on this book as a study in the theology of Paul Tillich: (2) reflections on this book as a link between Tillich and current feminist-womanist theologies; and (3) some reflections on this book from the standpoint of my recent work as chair of the Presbyterian Committee on Human Sexuality.

I.

Let it be said initially that this book is a fresh, creative, well-researched, and well-written work on a generally neglected theme in Tillich's theology. The book was a remarkable achievement by a thirty-one-year-old scholar who was still in the process of completing his own program of graduate studies at Harvard. I spoke with Alec Irwin by telephone and confirmed that this book began as an M.Div. thesis at Union Seminary in New York. (He actually began this book as a seminar paper in a Tillich seminar led by Tom Driver.) The book belies the comments often made by Tillich scholars of my generation to the effect that "we do not need any more expository studies of Tillich." It reminds us that younger generations read texts in new ways and bring new questions and concerns to old texts. We have certainly seen this process at work with the changing cycles of interest in biblical studies. It is interesting to see how it applies to the theological work of Paul Tillich. This book shows an impressive familiarity with Tillich scholarship on

---

[1]Subtitle: *Paul Tillich and the Theology of the Erotic* (Minneapolis: Fortress Press, 1991).

both sides of the Atlantic, and is especially enhanced by a familiarity with French Tillich scholarship.

Irwin's book helped me understand better than I had before Tillich's lifelong interest in the concept of eros, and the rich and diverse ways in which Tillich saw the power of eros at work in the world. Irwin, in fact, reminds us that the concept of eros can be taken as a clue to Tillich's entire systematic theology. Scholars have known for years that there are different ways into Tillich's system, and we are all aware of studies that have found entries into Tillich's thought through ontology, existentialism, language, the theory of symbol, or the method of correlation. The truth is that what we take from Tillich is related to the questions we ask, and the priority of our own concerns. Productive as that has been for many of us, it also means we can overlook other rich themes in Tillich's thought. Irwin reminds us that Tillich's lifelong interest in eros is one of those rich themes.

Of the many things that this book taught me, I would here cite three things. First, the importance of the book *Love, Power, and Justice*[2] in the Tillich corpus. *Love, Power, and Justice* is one of Irwin's major sources in this study, along with *Morality and Beyond*. I have never done much with *Love, Power, and Justice*, basically because it has not been central to my own interest in Tillich. Irwin's book, however, will cause most Tillich scholars to revisit *Love, Power, and Justice* with a fresh curiosity, and especially for how Tillich treats both eros and agape in that work.

A second contribution is Irwin's analysis of Tillich's various critiques of Anders Nygren's famous book *Agape and Eros*.[3] Irwin gives us an insightful analysis of what was at stake between Tillich and Nygren, with their two ways of seeing the world, their two theological systems, and their two different ways of interpreting Agape, and Eros. Nygren, mirroring a Barthian theological perspective that dominated a whole generation,

---

[2]Tillich, *Love, Power, and Justice: Ontological Analyses and Ethical Applications*, Firth Lectures in Nottingham, England; Sprunt Lectures in Richmond, Virginia (New York: Oxford University Press, 1953).

[3]*Agape and Eros* originally was published in Sweden in 1930 and 1936 (parts 1 and 2 respectively); it was serially translated into English and published in Great Britain in 1932, 1938, and 1939 (part 1, part 2/1, part 2/2); finally, it was revised, retranslated in part, and published in 1953 (Philadelphia: Westminster Press).

saw *agape* and *eros* as "dangerous rivals." They "represent two streams that run throughout the whole history of religion, alternately clashing against one another and mingling with one another" (*Agape and Eros*, 205). Nygren saw agape as God's free gift, the heart of an authentically Christian life. Eros, by contrast, represents human love and striving, shaped by the beauty and worth of its object. Eros, argued Nygren, is tainted by human emotions and drives, and lacks the purity or selflessness of agape. It is *other* than agape.

Tillich's reply to Nygren was that any attempt to pit eros and agape against each other generally presupposes that eros is to be identified with *epithymia*, the desire for sexual satisfaction. Tillich stressed the ontological unity of love, and that both eros and agape can be shaped by the divine Spirit. This debate was more complex than I can discuss here, but suffice it to say that in reviewing and clarifying this debate Irwin makes a major contribution to twentieth-century ethical theory.

A third contribution is Irwin's clarification of Tillich's engagement with Freud, both negatively and positively. Although there is much in Freud that Tillich felt has significance for Christian theology, Tillich criticized Freud for not making a distinction between the human being's "essential and existential nature" (he felt that Freud had no vision of a healed or whole person) and also for holding such a puritanical and negative attitude toward sex (see *Systematic Theology* 2:54). Tillich's engagement with Freud was a more important part of his work on the self and sexuality than I had realized.

In my judgment the weakest part of Irwin's work is in chapter 4, when he writes about Tillich's personal life. It is true that the disclosures about Tillich's marriage and private life which came through the two books of Hannah Tillich cannot be dismissed when one considers the topic of Paul Tillich's theology of the erotic. Methodologically Irwin accepts Hannah Tillich's appraisal of their life journey, and uses Hannah's expressions of pain and disappointment to criticize Tillich for not having dealt with this unhappy marriage with more integrity by dissolving that relationship with a divorce. Having investigated this sad and complex dimension of Tillich's life myself some years ago, and having contributed to the literature on it,[4] I recognize there are many

---

[4]See "Morality and Beyond: Tillich's Ethics in Life and in Death," in John

different ways to interpret that rather sad marital journey, and certainly there are different ways to understand Tillich's relationship with various female friends during his adult life. Rollo May and Ann Ulanov, for example, treat Tillich with more charity than does Hannah Tillich, and note that Tillich's caring friendships with women had integrity and respect, and were affirming for the persons involved.[5] Hannah Tillich had special relationships and liaisons of her own, and it is not clear that their marital relationship is a case of black-and-white judgments. Their pilgrimmage clearly involved pain on both sides, and their marriage was definitely not a conventional American middle-class marriage. I remain convinced that no good has come to anyone as a result of Hannah Tillich's angry book.

Although Irwin criticizes Tillich for his personal style and for the pain he caused Hannah, he does not use this analysis to negate the richness of Tillich's thought about eros as a factor in our ways of knowing, in our creative endeavors, and in the many forms of human relationships. That, I believe, is to his credit.

II.

It needs to be stressed, however, that this book is only partially about Paul Tillich. It is basically a book about the concept of eros, both as this idea was interpreted by Tillich but also about how eros is such a major theme with current feminist and womanist theologians. Irwin has been much engaged with Carter Heyward, with the black poet Audre Geraldine Lorde, with Rita Brock, Haunani-Kay Trask, Alice Walker, Beverly Harrison, and Dorothée Sölle. He is deeply persuaded that these feminist

---

J. Carey, ed., *Tillich Studies: 1975*, Second North American Consultation on Paul Tillich Studies (Tallahassee FL: The Consultation, Department of Religion, Florida State University, 1975) 104-15; and "Life on the Boundary: The Paradoxical Models of Tillich and Pike," *The Duke Divinity School Review* 42/3 (Fall 1977): 149-64.

[5]See May's *Paulus: Reminescenses of Friendship* (New York: Harper & Row, 1973) and Ulanov's "Between Anxiety and Faith: The Role of the Feminine in Tillich's Theological Thought," in J. A. K. Kegley, ed., *Paul Tillich on Creativity* (Lanham MD: University Press of America, 1989).

writers, poets, and theologians have in fact laid the groundwork for a new theology based on the power of eros. He notes that

> In the case of Christian theology, affirming Eros means breaking with ideas and attitudes that have been portrayed as cornerstones of Christian doctrine. Yet the alternative to this transformation of traditional attitudes and discourses is insolarity and stagnation, the admission that Christianity can no longer offer a word of life to the world but can only deny and withdraw from it. (191)

As Carter Heyward notes, erotic empowerment and erotic connectedness is the only basis of our hope for the world.[6] For this new feminist vision eros is joy, a source of knowledge, an essential ingredient in all relationships, a cosmic force, and a motivation for political action. Irwin agrees that this will be the theological model of the future. He notes:

> The future of Christian theology will be decisively influenced by the unfolding of the Eros concept and by the ability (or inability) of traditional theological structures to adapt themselves to new understandings of the role of the erotic in our lives as individuals and as communities. (191)

Scholars and theologians who are sympathetic to this "paradigm shift" will appreciate Irwin's book; those who are not will have some difficulty embracing it. A major unresolved issue is whether or not modern thought about eros still needs the corrective power of agape. Eros uncontrolled still has a capacity for exploitation. It is interesting that the call for a full embracing of eros comes from a lesbian theologian, who may be presuming that female erotic connectedness can be free of abuse or exploitation. Heterosexual dynamics, however, may still need to link eros with agape.

Irwin feels that for those who for any reason have difficulty in understanding the language and vision of this new feminist-womanist model, Tillich's theology provides an alternative foundation to see these same visions and come to essentially the same conclusions. In this way Irwin's work is one of the most important efforts yet made to show the linkage of Tillich's theology with the new feminist-womanist paradigm.

---

[6]*Touching our Strength: the Erotic as Power and the Love of God* (San Francisco: Harper & Row, 1989) 18.

III.

I came to Irwin's book, however, not just as a Tillich scholar, but as one who invested the major part of my professional energy for several years on sexuality issues. As I mentioned above, I served from 1987 to 1991 as chair of the Presbyterian National Committee on Human Sexuality. In that process I learned more about sexuality than I wanted to know; I was also propelled front and center into acrimonious Presbyterian and ecumenical debates about the nature and meaning of human sexuality. The Presbyterian majority report entitled "Keeping Body and Soul Together: Sexuality, Spirituality, and Social Justice" has sold more than 100,000 copies; that is a testimony to the interest in sexuality and spirituality. That experience certainly stretched my awareness of the complexities of sexuality in American culture. It is true that eros and sexuality are not identical, but they are closely related. On the basis of my recent experience I will make three observations about Tillich's thought about eros with reference to human sexuality.

1. On the whole Tillich was quite theoretical and abstract in his reflections on eros. He was preoccupied with the relationship between agape and eros, and the unity of the four different components of love. To read Tillich on eros reminds us that he was essentially a theologian and not an ethicist. (This is a little embarrassing to confess since one of my books on Tillich was entitled *Being and Doing: Paul Tillich as Ethicist.*[7])

2. For all of what Tillich saw at stake in the tension between agape and eros, he did not comment upon patriarchy as an ideology, nor did he comment upon heterosexism as an ideology that is so powerful in the shaping of gender roles in our society. From the standpoint of sexual quandaries in today's society we also have to note that Tillich did *not* write about sexual abuse, about special problems of gays and lesbians, about clergy sexual abuse, about the problems of the sexuality of handicapped persons or of older adults, nor about reproductive technologies. One can draw some inferences about these matters from Tillich's writings, but we need to be reminded that some of the specific areas of

---

[7](Macon GA: Mercer University Press, 1987).

sexual pain and exploitation in our society were not basically on Tillich's agenda.

3. Tillich recognized problems that are intrinsic to conventional middle-class marriage, but did not criticize marriage as it is currently understood by feminists as hierarchical, male-supportive, and linked with patriarchy and capitalism. Tillich was a powerful force, however, in trying to interject into Christian thought a positive alternative to the negativity about sexuality that has come through the tradition. He furthermore linked eros with concerns for justice, and stood against all those persons who would want to make of eros and sexuality something shameful or simple. He reminded us of its complexity, of its power, and of its redemptive capacities. In these ways he was ahead of his time, and we are in his debt.

IV.

I closed Irwin's book with a fresh sense of Tillich's boldness, imagination, and courage as a theologian, and also with an appreciation of Irwin's empathy for feminist issues. Tillich's voice is one of few from his generation from whom we can still learn regarding the creative, life-affirming power of eros. I am grateful that women have taken up this quest, and I support the theological transformation they seek. Irwin's study reminds us that Tillich is indeed a man for many seasons, and I am indebted to Irwin for his impressive and in-depth analysis.

Chapter 7

THE CONCEPT OF CREATION IN PAUL TILLICH, LANGDON GILKEY, AND SALLIE MCFAGUE

Why is there something and not nothing?
          —Martin Heidegger, after Leibniz, after Parmenides

To religious believers the doctrine of creation is much more than a story intended to satisfy human curiosity about how everything began. Its import goes much deeper, for it speaks directly to a common human concern about whether there are any realistic grounds for hope in the meaning of our lives and of the universe.   —John F. Haught

When I attended my first Templeton Foundation workshop on science and religion in Tallahassee, Florida, in January 1997 I was struck with the discussions about creation which are afoot in modern science. The debate between advocates of the "Big Bang" theory of creation and those who hold to a slower evolving process of creation were fascinating to listen to but not always easy to understand. Continued papers and deliberations on these themes at the second Templeton conference in Toronto in July 1997 made me aware of the complexity of this discussion and also raised in my mind the question of what theologians have to contribute to this discussion. If science probes the origins of our created order, just what do theologians add to those deliberations? It was on that basis that I decided to look more carefully at three Christian twentieth-century theologians and ask how they understand the nature and meaning of creation.

The theologians I have chosen to examine are Paul Tillich, considered by many to be Protestantism's most influential twentieth-century theologian; Langdon Gilkey, Shailer Mathews Professor of Theology emeritus at the University of Chicago; and Sallie McFague, former Carpenter Professor of Theology and former dean at the Vanderbilt Divinity School (now emeritus). These three theologians reflect differences of age, culture, and gender, and give us examples of three different ways of interpreting creation. The choice of these three is somewhat arbitrary, but is based on the fact of Tillich's enormous influence both in Europe and America; Gilkey's longtime scientific interests and writings on the doctrine of creation; and McFague's creative feminist analysis of the earth as God's body. If this were an academic course rather than a book chapter we could also comment on Karl Barth's writings on creation, the vision of Teilhard de Chardin, and the writings of Karl Rahner, Jürgen Moltmann, Richard Russell, and Ian Barbour. That is just a reminder that theological reflections on creation are broader than what we can deal with in this chapter.

I begin these reflections with three preliminary observations. (1) In the last analysis one cannot separate out views about creation without identifying in some broader way how one understands the relationship of religion and science. Ian Barbour begins his impressive volume *Religion in an Age of Science* (1990) by noting four ways of relating science and religion: conflict, independence, dialogue, and integration.[1] The *conflict* view implies seeing these two ways of knowing as hostile and incompatible with each other. The *independence* view maintains that there are different aspects of reality and that science examines some of those and religion probes others. The *dialogue* perspective encourages some mutual engagement, and encourages theological responses to issues raised by scientific inquiry. The *integration* viewpoint tries to bring together the insights of science and religion through models of natural theology, some type of theology of nature (one thinks here of Teilhard de Chardin) or some aspect of process theology. An example of this latter work of process theology would be found in the volume by Charles Birch and John B. Cobb, Jr., *The Liberation of Life*.[2] This is just a reminder that

---

[1] Ian G. Barbour, *Religion in an Age of Science* (San Francisco: Harper & Row, 1990). These same four perspectives are also utilized by John Haught in *Science and Religion* (New York: Paulist Press, 1995). Haught uses the terms conflict, contrast, and confirmation.

[2] *The Liberation of Life: From the Cell to the Community* (Cambridgeshire and New York: Cambridge University Press, 1981; repr.: Denton TX: Environmental Ethics Books, 1990).

where theologians come out on their reflections on creation is generally related to their deeper assumptions of how these two modes of inquiry relate to each other.

A second caveat is that this present essay is written from a Christian perspective. I recognize that other faith traditions have their own way of reflecting on creation, but it is beyond the purview of this essay to introduce the complexities of interfaith discussion. It is complex enough to consider three major Christian thinkers.

My third preliminary observation is that the doctrine of creation is often used as the pivotal doctrine in expressing the entire Christian faith. Gilkey points out that since so many churches have used the so-called Apostle's Creed, even laypersons are accustomed to the affirmation that God is "maker of heaven and earth," and from that affirmation come concerns not only about beginnings but also about providence, evil, and the meaning of life in general. In preparing a study like this, therefore, one has to be limited and judicious lest these reflections expand into a total exposition of Christian faith.

I.

Let us begin our consideration by turning to Paul Tillich. Our basic source will be volume 1 of Tillich's *Systematic Theology*, published in 1951 and probably the clue to everything else that Tillich ever wrote. It is worth pointing out, however, that Tillich had a longtime interest in the relationship of religion and science. Many people know his famous "Reply to Einstein," published in his *Theology of Culture* (1959),[3] in which he faulted Einstein for being too literal in his understanding of a personal god. Few people are aware, however, that before Tillich came to America he published in Germany in 1923 a volume entitled *Das System der Wissenschaften nach Gegenständen und Methoden*, which in English translation was entitled *The System of the Sciences according to*

---

[3]*Theology of Culture*, ed. Robert C. Kimball (New York: Oxford University Press, 1959).

Objects and Methods.[4] He divided his perspective on the sciences into the
sciences of thought (math, logic, phenomenology); the sciences of being
(physics and chemistry); Gestalt sciences (biology, psychology, and
sociology); the sequence sciences (historical analysis); and the sciences
of spirit (or human sciences), in which he places philosophy, theology,
and metaphysics. I mention this volume here to remind us that Tillich had
explored various facets of science and human knowledge and their
methods twenty-eight years before publication of volume 1 of his
Systematic Theology.[5]

In volume 1 of his *Systematic Theology* (*ST*), Tillich discusses the
doctrine of creation within the broader context of the concept of God. He
links the question of God with the questions of being and stresses the
symbolic nature of all religious language. He notes that virtually all
religions have pointed to some ultimate reality which is apart from this
world and our lives. The issue is how we name that reality and how we
know anything about it. He notes the patterns of polytheism in primitive
religions and the different aspects of monotheism: *monarchic monotheism,*
which one sees in the Bible; *mystical monotheism,* in which "the element
of ultimacy swallows the element of concreteness" (*ST* 1:226); *exclusive
monotheism,* expressed in the commandment that the god of Israel is a
"jealous God." Tillich feels that monotheism implies a principle of
justice. He eventually comments on *Trinitarian monotheism,* which he
says has nothing to do with how three can be one and one can be three.

_____

[4]Trans. Paul Wiebe (Lewisburg PA: Bucknell University Press, 1981).
Wiebe's translation may be indebted to an earlier translation (listed in OCLC as
an undated typescript) by Emile Grünberg that was in part revised by James
Luther Adams.

[5]*The System of the Sciences according to Objects and Methods* is not so
much an assessment of the natural sciences as it is an attempt to develop a
taxonomy of human knowledge. Tillich was concerned to justify the language of
theology and philosophy as a legitimate part of human knowledge and understanding. For more on Tillich's intention in this work, see Paul Wiebe, "From
System to Systematics: The Origin of Tillich's Theology," in *Kairos and Logos:
Studies in the Roots and Implications of Tillich's Theology,* ed. John J. Carey
(Macon GA: Mercer University Press, 1978) 109-20.

He notes that "the Trinitarian problem is the problem of the unity between ultimacy and concreteness in the living God" (*ST* 1:228).

Deriving from monotheism are three mythic visions or tendencies: (1) to hypostatize divine qualities like Wisdom, Word, and Glory, so that they are felt to be ontological realities; (2) the depiction of angels, represented biblically as divine messengers; and (3) the notion of a messiah or deliverer, who is a divine-human figure through whom God works. I mention this to remind us that what one says about creation is related to some of these broader aspects of what we know or can say about the revelatory nature of the divine. Among other options, Tillich notes that in the Christian tradition we have seen arguments for monistic naturalism, pluralistic naturalism, evolutionary deism, metaphysical dualism, and idealistic monism. This reminds us that our theological heritage is diverse indeed. Tillich, in my judgment, could be called an "ecstatic monist," but further elaboration of that is beyond our interests here.

Tillich starts with the assumption that there is a ground of being or power of being that undergirds all of life. He does not deduce this from any scientific data; he just assumes it. This reality is richer and more subtle than the God of theism. Indeed, theology must point to the "God beyond theism."[6] He assumes that although the sciences (particularly physics and astronomy) can probe the origins of the cosmos, they cannot *per se* help us on the question of life's meaning and its end. In his discussion of "God as creating" he notes that the doctrine of creation does not describe an event (*ST* 1:252); it rather points to the situation of creatureliness and to its correlate, the divine creativity. The doctrine of creation in Tillich's judgment begins with the assumption that creation is not an accident but a purposive and deliberate action of God. It carries within it an affirmation of some sustaining power that originates creation, sustains creation, and directs creation.

In this context, Tillich examines the historic Christian claim that God created the world or worlds *ex nihilo*. He recognizes that this has been a theological and not a scientific assertion. He notes that historically this

---

[6]This is discussed in *Systematic Theology* 1:245-49, but more fully in *The Courage to Be* (New Haven CT: Yale University Press, 1952) 182-90.

doctrine arose to protect Christianity against any claim of ultimate dualism or any theological system that would limit God's power (for example, Socinianism in the sixteenth century). But if God alone fashioned the world or worlds, and if the creation was good, how can we understand a sense of fallenness in the creation, or the human experience of the tragic? He notes that the doctrine of creation *ex nihilo* expresses two fundamental truths. The first is that the tragic character of existence is not rooted in the creative ground of being; it does not belong to the nature of things. (This is the Augustinian answer to the problem of evil.) Tillich argues that "the tragic is conquered by the presence of being itself within the finite" (*ST* 1:254). The second truth in this historic doctrine is that there is an element of nonbeing in creatureliness; this gives insight into the necessity of death and into the potentially (but not necessity) of the tragic. We live our lives, therefore, in an imperfect world. We are finite and alienated from the ground of our being.

It is interesting that Tillich links the concept of Creation so closely with his understanding of the Fall. This is essentially the problem of how one moves from a good and purposive creation to fallen and broken existence. Tillich's discussion of this point deserves further elaboration that I can give it in this chapter. Suffice it to say that Tillich stresses the difference between human essence and human existence. He believes God has brought humankind into being and has bestowed upon humankind the gift of finite freedom (*ST* 1:255) and that in pursuit of this freedom, we actualize ourselves outside of the creative ground of the divine life. He notes that "creaturely freedom is the point at which creation and the fall coincide" (*ST* 1:256).

Tillich also addresses the complex question of creation and time. He leans more towards a "Big Bang" theory without discussing this in detail, but reflects on the puzzling problem (which goes back to Augustine) as to whether there was some kind of divine time before the world comes into being, or whether our sense of time begins with creation. He knows that from a theological viewpoint this is pure speculation. It has within it the problem of how we speak about the "divine eternity." Basically, however, humans have enough to worry about as we think of our personal time of existence, shaped as it is by alienation and the threat of nonbeing.

Two other observations might be made about Tillich as he works through the notion of creation. The first is that for him humanity is the *telos* of creation, and our link with the divine ground has been expressed in the metaphor that we are made in the "image of God" (*ST* 1:258). It is our rational structure, he argues, that is at the heart of the metaphor of being made in the "image of God." This supports the notion of the "hierarchy of powers of being," or the "Great Chain of Being" (cf. *ST* 1:233).

Tillich cautions us, however, about thinking of creation as a past event. He envisions a power that directs, sustains, and enhances the world. He notes that "God is essentially creative, and therefore he is creative in every moment of temporal existence, giving the power of being to everything that has being out of the creative ground of the divine life" (*ST* 1:262). The theological doctrines of Immanence and Transcendence are spatial symbols of this affirmation.

Tillich is confident enough about the reality of the divine that he says symbolically we can embrace a doctrine of Providence. Providence for Tillich means God's permanent activity, and that God "never is a spectator; [God] always directs everything towards its fulfillment" (*ST* 1:266). The idea of providence, of course, has both individual and social connotations, and oftentimes our embracing of providence is a paradoxical affirmation made in spite of personal and or social tragedies.

In sum, Tillich offers a comprehensive sense of creation which includes all of the world (and worlds) being undergirded by the power of being. He does not, interestingly enough, draw on scientific models to support his claim that our world has order and purpose. He was not an empiricist. He did not privilege scientific language or data: as he argued in his 1923 book later translated as *The System of the Sciences according to Objects and Methods*,[7] the natural sciences are but one of many ways of knowing, and both what science examines and its methods are limited. His theory of a structure of being, or power of being, was not set against

---

[7]Trans. Paul Wiebe (Lewisburg PA: Bucknell University Press, 1981). Original: *Das System der Wissenschaften nach Gegenständen und Methoden* (Göttingen: Vandenhoeck & Ruprecht, 1923).

the newer cosmologies (as Ian Barbour describes them)[8] or against Chaos theory.

Tillich was, in short, a Christian theologian. Scientists might fault him for simply assuming what scientists and philosophers seek to prove. He recognized that the biblical metaphors for God as Creator, King, Father, and Shepherd are symbolic, but he did not explore how those terms have been used to support a patriarchal Christianity. He was more interested in ontological structures than in the paradoxes of nature. If one can start where Tillich starts, his work is impressive and reassuring. The problem is that fewer people these days are willing to start where Tillich started.

II.

We turn now to the thought of Langdon Brown Gilkey, who has probed the interaction of science and religion for most of his professional career. Gilkey was born in China in 1919 of missionary parents and was imprisoned there during World War II. He returned to the United States to complete a doctorate at Union Theological Seminary in New York, where he worked under both Reinhold Niebuhr and Paul Tillich. Upon graduation he was appointed to the faculty at the Vanderbilt Divinity School and left in 1969 to join the faculty of the University of Chicago where he spent most of his career. After retiring from Chicago, Gilkey spent several years at the University of Virginia Department of Religious Studies. He was called as an expert witness by the American Civil Liberties Union at the prominent "creationist" trial in Little Rock Arkansas, December 7-9, 1981. Portions of his testimony at that trial have been anthologized in other sources, but Gilkey tells the full story in his book, *Creationism on Trial*.[9] (As a result of that trial and certainly related to Gilkey's testimony about science and religion, the federal court in Little

---

[8]See Ian G. Barbour, *Religion in an Age of Science*, the Gifford Lectures 1989–1990 (San Francisco: Harper & Row, 1990) 135-40, where he talks about the "anthropic principle" and new cosmological models of chance and necessity.

[9]*Creationism on Trial: Evolution and God at Little Rock* (Minneapolis: Winston Press, 1985).

Rock struck down an Arkansas statute that required creationism to be taught along with evolutionary theory in the public schools of Arkansas.)

The range of Gilkey's interests in science and religion can be seen in the publication of his *The Maker of Heaven and Earth*, a full-length study of the idea of creation;[10] of his *Religion and the Scientific Future*;[11] his volume *Creationism on Trial*; and his *Nature, Reality, and the Sacred*.[12] Gilkey has participated in many national consultations on religion and science and has lectured at various Templeton Foundation conferences. There is naturally some overlap in the different books Gilkey has published, but there is no doubt that he has been a major player from the theological side in the modern discussion of science and religion. Interestingly enough, Gilkey has been sharply critical of the work of modern science, especially regarding its lack of interest in the researcher as person and in its inadequate epistemology. I will have more to say about that shortly. He has definitely been more engaged with scientific endeavors than Tillich was.

The full scope of Gilkey's thought on the doctrine of creation and its related implications for science and religion is beyond what I can consider in this chapter. I do, however, want to profile several distinctive contributions that Gilkey has made to the discussion.

Gilkey approaches this complex topic with the full awareness of the long history of controversy between science and religion. He notes that this controversy has been fueled over many years by the assumptions of each side that it had some special clear, even "objective," truth about the nature of the universe and our place in it. Broadly speaking, this has been the conflict between scientism and biblical literalism. Gradually, however,

---

[10]Title-page subtitle: *A Study of the Christian Doctrine of Creation*, Christian Faith series (Garden City NY: Doubleday, 1959; paperback: Anchor Books/Doubleday, 1965). The subtitle on the cover of the popular paperback edition is *The Christian Doctrine of Creation in the Light of Modern Knowledge*.

[11]Subtitle: *Reflections on Myth, Science, and Theology*, Deems Lectures at New York University, 1967 (New York: Harper & Row, 1970; reprinted as Rose 2: Macon GA: Mercer University Press, 1981).

[12]Subtitle: *The Nexus of Science and Religion*, Theology and the Sciences series (Minneapolis: Fortress Press, 1993).

with the rise of historical criticism in biblical studies and the increasing awareness that the books of the Bible contain various literary genres, Gilkey notes that the religious community (not all, but much of it) came to change its understanding of what constitutes religious truth. Gilkey notes that

> The change referred to is that from the understanding of religious truths as made up of propositions containing, among other things, divinely revealed "information" on almost any topic of interest, to the understanding of them as a system of symbols which make no authoritative assertions about concrete matters of fact. Within the last century the mythical language of religion, which, when systematically reflected upon, becomes theological discourse, has relinquished the claim to be able to make indicative statements about matters of fact; . . . [13]

Science for its part also had a rigid understanding of its work about origins and the direction of the universe. Gilkey notes that all of science from Galileo through Newton, Priestly, Ray, Dalton, Boyle, and others assumed

> (a) That the fundamental forms and structures of present natural things had been permanently established by a recent act of creation, and thus that the laws concerning these permanent forms of species were universal and timeless. (b) That these permanent forms made up an intelligible system in relation to their world because they were purposefully or teleologically preadapted to each other and to their environment by the wisdom and benevolence of the Creator in a glorious harmony of ends and means.[14]

Gilkey argues that the modern age has certainly brought new perspectives to science as well as to religion. That is what has set the stage for the modern debate.

In terms of our different models of approaching religion and science, the early work of Gilkey might be considered as an example of the "contrast" model. That is to say, he respects the work of science but

---

[13]*Religion and the Scientific Future*, 4.
[14]*Religion and the Scientific Future*, 11.

argues that science and religion inquire about different aspects of truth and reality. Science, in his opinion, is legitimately concerned about the origins of things, the structure of matter, and the complexity of the created order. It answers questions of the "what" and "when" with as much objectivity as it can. Religion for Gilkey (perhaps we should say, for him specifically the Christian faith) asks a different set of questions as it ponders the created order. Religion asks about the "why" of creation, and asks that question with personal intensity. Gilkey notes that we ask the ultimate questions with a distinctly personal reference. We are raising the question of origins because we are asking about an ultimate security, the meaning and destiny of our own existence. Our personal stake in the matter, in effect, prompts us to ask the metaphysical question of being in an "existential" form.[15] In other words, our interest in creation from a religious standpoint is not that we can or should second guess scientific theories, but whether or not we can trust that creation has some meaning. Gilkey notes that

> The question of the meaning and destiny of our present life can only be answered if we have confidence in the fundamental goodness of life as promising fulfillment; and such confidence in the promise of life is possible only if we have some basis for trust in the source of all being. . . . Thus in asking the religious question "Who created the world?" men are not so curious about how or when the universe came to be as they are deeply concerned about the goodness and meaning of their life. . . . [16]

There has been an interesting evolution in Gilkey's thought about creation from the publication of his *Maker of Heaven and Earth* in 1959 up to the publication of his *Nature, Reality, and the Sacred* in 1993. Gilkey's earlier book treats multiple theological ideas related to the concept of creation: the meaning of life, evil, time, and the early Christian assertion that creation was *ex nihilo*. His entire work, however, reflects a broader theological mood of the late 1950s, namely, the period of biblical theolo-

---

[15]See *Maker of Heaven and Earth*, 27.
[16]*Maker of Heaven and Earth*, 29-30 (22-23 in paperback edition).

gy that sought to interpret the Bible as a record of God's "mighty acts," and saw the great themes of the Bible as Creation, Covenant, Christ, Church, and Consummation.[17] Gilkey, while even then acknowledging that the mysteries of creation were beyond theological verification, spoke with confidence that the Judeo-Christian tradition was a history through which we could see "the mighty acts of God in history."

In *Nature, Reality, and the Sacred* (1993), however, Gilkey moves more toward a position of a natural theology. He talks less about God's mighty acts in history and more about signs or "traces" of God found in the natural order. In making this shift, Gilkey moves from the "contrast" position to a more integrative viewpoint. There is a difference, by the way, between a theology of nature and a natural theology. A theology of nature, as Ian Barbour points out, does not start from science, but rather from a religious tradition based on religious experience and historical revelation. Natural theology strives for an integrative model which will work for both science and religion, such as evaluating deism or the work of Teilhard and Whitehead. Gilkey represents more of a theology of nature.

Attempting now to integrate science and religion through a concept of nature, Gilkey argues that our created order provides us with "traces" of God. Just what are these "traces?"

(1) First of all, Gilkey argues, nature discloses itself as power. There is a driving power in nature that can convert itself into energy and into matter. This power is for human beings an awesome reality that we experience not only in things around us but within ourselves and our power to be. This power gives us the ground for our own existence and it manifests itself on different levels and modes of being. Gilkey here seems to be close to pantheism, and, like Henri Bergson, points to an "*elan vital*." Nature's power generates life in the world. It is awesome, and points us to the divine.

(2) The awareness of power is accompanied by a demand, signaled by law or obligation and acknowledged by human obedience and service. Gilkey notes that no one escapes this demand and its accompaniment in

---

[17]See Bernard W. Anderson's various writings on this theme, esp. his *Understanding the Old Testament* (Englewood Cliffs NJ: Prentice Hall, 1957).

what we call "conscience."[18] One is reminded here of Immanuel Kant's famous stress on duty.

(3) Gilkey notes that nature exhibits an order which is apprehended universally by the humans participating in it and witnessing to it. Here Gilkey is close to the classic argument from design. He notes that order paradoxically includes spontaneity and openness. It appears at different levels or dimensions of nature.

(4) Fourth, this order has implications for "what we ought to do." It provides us with a hierarchy of values in which we can discern the call to justice and goodness. He does not develop this into a natural law theory, but he leans in that direction.

(5) A fifth trace of divine intent in creation is the affinity of the creation with and for human life. Although Gilkey does not use this term, here he is close to what many scientists call "the Anthropic Principle," which is a way of describing the universe (however it came into being) as "user friendly" to human beings, and thus supports the claim of a divine intent in creation.

(6) Finally, in what he calls the strangest trace of the divine, Gilkey notes the intertwining of life with death throughout nature. It is strange, he notes, that death is perceived as our ultimate threat yet intertwines itself with life and with value. How can we understand God, he asks (not to mention human values) if both are separated radically from the reality of death? Nature in its normal flow deals with beginnings and endings, life and death, positive and negative, being and nonbeing. Meditating on these mysteries, Gilkey feels that in this rhythm we can discern yet another trace of divine intent.

Where then does our consideration of Gilkey leave us? In *Maker of Heaven and Earth*, he reminds us that the concept of creation is the most fundamental of all for Christian theology. He contrasts the different kinds of questions that grow out of scientific inquiry and the religious search for personal meaning. He recognizes the place of myth in religious language, and draws from Tillich about the symbolic nature of religious language. He is more interested in the history and philosophy of science

---

[18]See *Nature, Reality, and the Sacred*, 183.

than Tillich was. He engages such contemporary cosmologists as Heinz Pagels, Carl Sagan, Stephen Weinberg, Richard Dawkins, and Frank Tipler, and faults them all for having a much-too-simplified epistemology. They all ignore, he feels, the critical philosophy of Immanuel Kant, since they all claim some "objective" knowledge for their claims. This has led, he fears, to an arrogance in many scientists about their assertions. That has made dialogue difficult in some contexts and impossible in others. It is also why philosophy must always be a third partner in the science and religion dialogue.[19] In his effort to develop a consistent theology of nature, Gilkey has some affinities with such philosophers as Richard Swinburne, F. R. Tennant, and John Leslie. His later work has some parallels with Sallie McFague, and it is to her work that we now turn.

III.

Sallie McFague, as I noted earlier, is the former Carpenter Professor of Theology (now emeritus) at the Vanderbilt Divinity School. She has completed a sequence of four books which deal with language, metaphors, ecology, and nature. These include *Metaphorical Theology: Models of God in Religious Language* (1982), *Models of God: Theology for an Ecological, Nuclear Age* (1987), *The Body of God: An Ecological Theology* (1993), and *Super, Natural Christians: How We Should Love Nature* (1997).[20] McFague is important for our considerations because she brings a female perspective on the theological language of creation, and because she—far more than either Tillich or Gilkey—is interested in an ecological theology. Perhaps more so than either Gilkey or Tillich, McFague also seeks to address creation from the standpoint of the threats of a nuclear age. She describes herself as a "Christian, a theologian, a feminist, and an ecologist."[21]

---

[19]See Gilkey's article, "Whatever Happened to Immanual Kant?" in his *Nature, Reality, and the Sacred*, 43-58.

[20]All four books were published by Fortress Press, the first two at Philadelphia, the last two at Minneapolis.

[21]*The Body of God*, 13-14.

McFague's chapter on cosmology in *The Body of God* opens up many vistas of her thought. She criticizes the traditional Western interpretation of creation by noting that it stresses the interdependence of all things; that as human beings we are part of an ongoing community of being; that we are kin to all creatures; that the cosmos is all of one piece; and that humanity is the most advanced form of life that we know. As this story has been told, however, it has been intertwined with social and political interpretations. It certainly has been insensitive to nature, inasmuch as it stresses that human beings should have dominion over nature. So it is time, McFague argues, that we offer an entirely different perspective on creation and explore some models that can renew and refocus our sense of life. She notes that the traditional anthropocentric creation story has been used to support the primacy of males, and basically has essentialized concepts of maleness and femaleness. But she says:

> What if we changed our perspective from its narrow focus on the one ideal human (male) body as the base of the model, to a cosmic focus so that what came to mind when we thought of body was bodies—in other words not sameness but *difference*?[22]

A new model for understanding creation might help us develop "a new eye for difference, a new sense for perceiving difference, and tell us something about diversity in proportions and in detail unlike anything we have known before."[23] The new story we need to develop, she argues, is first of all a cosmology that will give us a unified view of reality. On the whole, she is supportive of some form of the "Big Bang" theory, and supports scientific data about the process of evolution.

McFague feels that any new perspective on creation must include a more intense and personal view of knowing and doing. It will require more reflection about epistemology. Here she notes the importance of "attention epistemology" which is "listening, paying attention to another, the other, in itself, for itself."[24] We might call this mode of knowing

---

[22]*The Body of God*, 37.
[23]*The Body of God*, 39.
[24]*The Body of God*, 49.

"attentiveness," or gaining a greater sensitivity to that which is about us. Feminist epistemology stresses the importance of gender and the fact of great differences in the human community. It points us to care of the earth and concern for a positive ecosystem. It invites us to see with "loving eyes." This new story shaped by feminist sensitivities is imperative because of the sad state of our planet. Our lamentable condition, she argues, has derived from our traditional sense of domination over nature.

It should be clear that McFague shares with Gilkey and Tillich the notion that theological reflection on creation does not provide us with scientific facts, but is a way of talking about meaning and direction for human life. Her new model is that we think of the world as the "Body of God." This new model, she argues, is more consistent with the view of reality in our time, and is more useful as a construct for human living. It is ecological in the sense that it gives us new visions of space and place. Sin, she notes, might well be our refusal to accept our place in the universe or to distort our mutual relationship with each other or with animals or nature. Emphasis on the body of God helps us to be liberating, healing, and sharing in our sense of the earth and of life.

Let me underscore that McFague's use of the term "body of God" is not some ontological description, but a metaphor. This metaphor, she argues, results in a "personal and ecological way of reimagining the traditions of creation in terms compatible with contemporary science."[25] It is critical, she argues, that we understand creation as the continuing, dynamic, growing embodiment of God, "a body given life and power for the evolution of billions of diverse entities and creatures."

One of the themes McFague derives from her new creation model is an inclusive love for all, especially the oppressed, the outcast, and the vulnerable. The clue to her metaphor of the world as body of God is clearly the life, teachings, and death of Jesus of Nazareth. Her depiction and interpretation of Jesus is not so much that of the synoptic gospels, however, as it is based on the cosmic Christ, following the Pauline observations in the first chapter of Colossians.[26] Here she has some

---

[25]*The Body of God*, 156.

[26]The text in Colossians 1:15-16 reads: "He is the image of the invisible God,

interesting affinities with Matthew Fox and his work on creation spirituality, but she faults that movement for not adequately dealing with despair, tragedy, and hopelessness which characterize the lives of so many millions of people.

In sum, by offering a new creation story (or, we might say, by offering a different conceptual model), McFague reminds us

(1) of the interdependence and independence of all living things: men and women are equal under God and both are involved with nature;
(2) that we must live appropriately and responsibly within the scheme of things and be better stewards of the gifts of nature;
(3) that the divine promise of salvation (or "wholeness") is for all living things, not just for human beings;
(4) that responsible life entails solidarity with the oppressed; and
(5) that we have a special vocation to be stewards of life on earth and partners with God.[27]

All of these themes are expanded in her subsequent book, *Super, Natural Christians* (1997), subtitled *How We Should Love Nature*. McFague offers there a genuine theology of nature, and hence would be regarded in the "integrationist" perspective that Barbour mentions. The broad scope of her work is similar in intent to what Teilhard de Chardin developed in grand evolutionary scheme. Clearly, McFague goes beyond both Gilkey or Tillich in her incorporation of ecological, feminist, and liberationist motifs related to creation.

IV.

All of these persons invited us to do deeper reflection on the concept of creation from the standpoint of a Christian understanding of the world. All deserve more detailed consideration than I can give them in this chapter. All would agree, however, that the concept of creation is a

---

the firstborn of all creation; for in him all things in heaven and on earth were created, things visible and invisible, whether thrones or dominions or rulers or powers—all things have been created through him and for him" (NRSV).
[27]*The Body of God*, 199-201.

critical issue in Christian consciousness, for from that concept we derive our senses of life, meaning, and vision. All agree that theologians ask different questions about the implications of creation than scientists ask, but they feel there is no sharp conflict between the fruits of scientific research and the interests of religion. The mystery of creation remains. Theologians cannot explain it. Neither can scientists.

I have learned much from the insights of these three theologians. Tillich's method of correlation seems to work well with science-and-religion issues just as it does in relating philosophy and theology. Tillich's emphasis that any serious theological reflection on creation must also stretch our concept of God is a major point. The differences he notes in his *Systematic Theology* (1:71-81) between "technical reason" and the "depth of reason" remind us that theories of epistemology are indeed present in discussions about science and religion.

Gilkey's attempt to develop a theology of nature is suggestive, as well as his assertion that philosophy is a vital third participant in today's discussions. Sallie McFague is bold in her search for new metaphors and a call for a more ecologically oriented theology.

For my part, I think contemporary theologians ought to read more in the area of new cosmologies, as these are articulated by Ian Barbour and Robert Russell, and track the discussion as it is reported in *Zygon* and other periodical literature. That betrays my own preference for the "Dialogue" model of this relationship. The questions raised in this dialogue are so important that it does not matter if our answers need constant revising.[28]

---

[28]The John Templeton Foundation has sponsored the preparation of an eighty-seven-page *Annotated Bibliography on the Relationship between the Physical Sciences and Spirituality* (Berkeley CA: Center for Theology and the Natural Sciences, 1995). This bibliography categorizes contributor's as scientists with theological training, scientists without theological training, theologians with scientific training, and theologians with scientific training. This bibliography is available from the Center for Theology and the Natural Sciences in Berkeley, California, and from most regional offices of the John Templeton Foundation.

Chapter 8

ARE THERE ANY ABSOLUTES LEFT? POSTMODERNISM AND THE CRISIS FOR TILLICH SCHOLARS

The struggle for the absolute in a secularized world is an inner process in the secularized realms. It is not imposed by religious aspirations but is man's reaction against being without a structure of meaning. The religions of the world must acknowledge this struggle and not destroy it by an arrogant dogmatism. They must open themselves to those who ask the question of the absolute with passion and unconditional seriousness, both inside and outside the churches.
　　　　　　　—Paul Tillich, *My Search for Absolutes*, 42

New discoveries are tough on old theories, and the newer theories that replace them are more exotic than ever.
　　　　—James E. Hutchingson, *Religion and the Natural Sciences*, 184

Every scholar who takes Paul Tillich seriously has a difficult time coming out of the great man's shadow. To be a Tillich scholar is to see the world in a particular way, understand theological language in a special way, understand the role and function of symbols in religious life and discourse, and certainly to understand many of the deeper meanings of Christianity in the twentieth century. Tillich wrote so much and opened up so many areas of thought for modern theology that most scholars who study his work are deeply shaped by his way of framing questions and providing answers. Since I wrote my doctoral dissertation on Tillich I have continued to be interested in Tillich scholarship, and it has been a tension for me to retain that interest while also personally moving on into other theological issues and viewpoints. This essay grows out of my own recent work in the literature of Postmodernism, much of which has been about as clear to me as reading Tillich's original German dissertation on Schelling. Like it or not, Postmodernism has profoundly shaped the modern intellectual climate and has aesthetic, literary, philosophical, and political components and implications. Because it seems so threatening to traditional religious claims and to theological work, one is tempted to push this movement aside and declare that it is yet another fad developed by the cultured despisers of religion. In the Tillichian spirit, however, I feel it is important that we look at this movement with seriousness, and ask how (if at all) it reorients us in theological scholarship and even in religious life.

I.

My reflections in this essay were originally inspired by Tom Bandy's call for papers for the 1997 North American Paul Tillich Society meeting. One of his suggested themes was the place of "the absolute" in Tillich's thought and in our own thought. Since much of Postmodernism speaks of "the dissolution of the absolute,"[1] I thought it might be interesting to examine once again Tillich's commitment to an absolute and then to assess the various claims of Postmodernists about our "new age." I turned to Tillich's *My Search for Absolutes*, published posthumously.[2] *My Search for Absolutes* was published in the "Credo Perspectives" series, planned and edited by Ruth Nanda Anshen. It was published in an edition that included drawings by Saul Steinberg, one of the creative abstract artists in the 1960s. This book has not drawn much attention from Tillich scholars, perhaps because it seems to recapture and refocus many of Tillich's earlier ideas. The book is made up of lectures Tillich gave at the University of Chicago Law School in the spring of 1965, and he intended to give them again as the Nobel Lectures at Harvard in the 1965–1966 academic year. His death precluded that second opportunity.

---

[1][Editor's note.] During the 1960s heyday of the so-called Death of God Movement, Paul van Buren canonized this phrase with his article "The Dissolution of the Absolute," *Religion in Life* 34 (Summer 1965): 334-42. But historically the phrase (and the idea it designates) probably is to be traced to Lorenz Oken (1779–1851) who conceived natural science as the science of the eternal transformation of God into the world, of *the dissolution of the Absolute into plurality*.

[2]Paul Tillich, *My Search for Absolutes*, with drawings by Saul Steinberg, Credo Perspectives, ed. Ruth Nanda Anshen (New York; Simon and Schuster, 1967; repr. as a Touchstone Book, 1984) 143 pages and with illustrations. The complete text is now online at <http://www.religion-online.org/cgi-bin/relsearchd. dll/showbook?item_id=1631>.

I want to begin my consideration of our topic by reflecting on Tillich's book, *My Search for Absolutes*. This volume has four chapters, the first of which is an autobiographical essay, "What Am I? An Autobiographical Essay: Early Years." (This essay is of course very similar to his "Intellectual Biography" in the Kegley and Bretall volume, *The Theology of Paul Tillich*, and to his even earlier autobiographical essay, *On the Boundary*.[3]) This chapter 1 autobiography is helpful for those who are unfamiliar with Tillich's intellectual pilgrimage but offers little that is new for scholars who know Tillich's previous biographical essays. The heart of the book is in chapters 2, 3, and 4, entitled "Absolutes in Human Knowledge and the Idea of Truth"; "The Absolute and the Relative Element in Moral Decisions"; and "The Holy—the Absolute and the Relative in Religion."

Tillich believed that relativism and the spirit of autonomy were the great threats that plagued religious faith in the twentieth century. He was persuaded that against these sifting sands, metaphysical understanding and genuine religion needed to be rooted in the concept of the Absolute. The Absolute for Tillich is that ultimate reality and/or power that transcends all relativities. This Absolute gives the world purpose, direction, and meaning. It provides the underlying structure behind all human knowledge and reasoning. In chapter 2 he notes that

> the very concept of knowledge presupposes an absolute structure within the flux of relative knowledge. The human mind could not maintain its centeredness, its self-awareness, without something that remains absolute in the stream of changing relativities. Every act of knowledge confirms this powerful safeguard against getting lost in that stream. (70)

Even though people and cultures represent a wide variety of experiences and tradition, Tillich observes that

---

[3]Namely, *The Theology of Paul Tillich*, ed. Charles W. Kegley and Robert Walter Bretall, the Library of Living Theology 1 (New York: Macmillan, 1952) 370 pages; 2nd ed., rev. and ed. by Charles W. Kegley (New York: Pilgrim Press, 1982) xvi+432 pages. Tillich, *On the Boundary: An Autobiographical Sketch*, a revision, newly translated, of part 1 of the author's *The Interpretation of History* (New York; Scribner, 1966).

> There are several absolutes in the stream of these relative encounters.
> The first is the absolute that makes language possible. The second is the
> absolute that makes understanding possible. And the third is the absolute
> that makes truth possible. (72)

He notes that it is this conviction, this certainness of the absolute, that led
him to talk about ontological categories and ontological polarities. These
structures that undergird our human pilgrimage and all knowledge are
rooted in "being itself," which Tillich calls "the most fundamental of all
absolutes" (81). So we would say on Tillich's first major point that the
power of the absolute is what undergirds all of our human identity and
knowledge. He sometimes calls this the *Logos* structure of the world.

In the chapter that deals with the absolute and moral decisions
(chapter 3), Tillich speaks of a moral imperative that is unconditionally
valid. Why is that "moral imperative" important? Tillich answers,

> because it is our own true or essential being that confronts us in the
> moral command demanding something from us in our actual being with
> all its problems and distortions. If we act against this command from
> our true being, we violate ourselves. (95)

Tillich's language here is opaque, but his intention is clear. As finite
creatures we are linked to, and accountable to the Divine. The "moral
imperative" is a way of saying that the Divine calls us to responsibility.
Churches seek to remind us of this when we are admonished to do the
"Will of God." What does this moral imperative entail? Tillich suggests
three things:

> (1) That we acknowledge every person as a person. (One thinks here of
> Immanuel Kant.) This imperative ultimately underlies the principle of
> justice and eventually of righteousness;
> (2) the guiding by the power of Agape, which Tillich says is the
> absolute moral principle, the "star" above the chaos of relativism" (109);
> and
> (3) embracing of risk, which grows out of personal openness and all-
> important decision making. Risk is essential for deeper and more
> meaningful life; there is no growth without it.

Finally, Tillich argues that our awareness of the absolute leads us to
a sense of the holy. To use some characteristic Tillich language, he

argues that to experience the holy is to know "the absolute-itself." He draws a lot on Rudolph Otto in his discussion of this theme and notes that finally in religious awareness it is the Holy (or the Absolute) that transcends and judges every religion. The Holy exposes the demonization of religions and the claims of quasireligions. Although Tillich for most of his life could be regarded as a Christian apologist, in *My Search for Absolutes* he concludes that no religion can claim to be absolute (141).

All religions carry with them the impact of local cultures and reflect various parochialisms. Tillich, who was more interested in Judaism and Christianity than in other nontheistic world religions, would say rather typically that all religions are symbolic structures that point beyond themselves. All, however, albeit imperfectly, point to the *Absolute*, to the *Ground of Being*.

II.

I confess that through much of my professional life, I have been molded by these Tillichian assumptions and categories. I have written articles defending the proposition that "Tillich is a man for all seasons," and that subsequent theological interpreters can still be guided by his work. Recently, however, I have begun to take more seriously those voices that maintain that we are now living in a "post-Tillichean period," just as many scholars have argued during the last thirty years that ours is really a "post-Christian" world. As early as 1981, Lonnie Kliever, in his book *The Shattered Specturm*,[4] commented on the passing of the Modern Era. Kliever, in his assessment of the modern theological situation would link Tillich with the assumptions of the Modera Era. The Modern Era, noted Kliever, has been concerned with

> the conflict of nature and person, subject and object, fact and value, certitude and doubt. But from this principal also flowed the modern world's distinctive achievements—experimental method, rational criticism, political freedom, individual autonomy, experiential religion. This "modern era" also sanctions those central institutions of the Modern Age—democracy, capitalism, and romantic marriage.[5]

---

[4]Lonnie D. Kliever, *The Shattered Specturm: A Survey of Contemporary Theology* (Atlanta: John Knox Press, 1981).
[5]Kliever, *The Shattered Specturm*, 197.

(We might bracket for our purposes the validity of Tillich's interest in romantic marriage, but the other themes and assumptions seem to be very close to Tillich's conceptual world.) Kliever goes on to say that "The modern Modern Age stood for the truimph of subjectivity, universality, and eminence in every field of human endeavor."[6]

Kliever, of course, was not the only one to recognize that we have been living through the shifting consciousness and coming into a new conceptual world. As already noted above, Paul van Buren, writing as early as 1965, described "the dissolution of the absolute."[7] Van Buren called this cultural transition a "sociopsychological" fact, and noted that in this new climate, metaphysical thought does not give us anything new to see. Most scholars recall that van Buren was associated with the Death of God movement in the mid 1960s, and that he operated from a linguistic-analytical philosophical viewpoint that sharply contrasted with Tillich on many points. Language of such words as "absolute reality" belong (in van Buren's judgment) to the world of the nineteenth century and not to the latter half of the twentieth century. (Tillich, in van Buren's view, appeared to be like Einstein, who spent the last forty years of his life seeking a unified field theory while virtually the whole discipline of physics was moving in other directions.)

Perhaps the most fundamental issue that has recast Tillich's world, however, has been the emergence of pluralism.[8] We speak much more now of studies of comparative cultures with all of their symbolisms and histories. We recognize—painfully for some of us, of course—the distinctive perspectives of gender, race, and social class on intellectual issues. We speak in theology as well as in biblical studies about "social

---

[6]Ibid.

[7]Paul van Buren, "The Dissolution of the Absolute," *Religion in Life* 34 (Summer 1965): 334-42.

[8]See, e.g., John Hick, *Problems of Religious Pluralism* (New York: St. Martin's Press, 1985); Lesslie Newbigin, *The Gospel in a Pluralistic Society* (Grand Rapids MI: Eerdmans, 1989); John Hick and Paul F. Knitter, *The Myth of Christian Uniqueness: Toward a Pluralistic Theology of Religions* (Mary Knoll NY: Orbis Press, 1987) esp. the chapters by Hick (16-36) and Langdon Gilkey (37-50); Hans Küng, *Theology for the Third Millennium* (New York: Doubleday, 1988) esp. 197-207 and 227-56. There are many nuances in the discussion of pluralism, but further explanation is beyond the scope of this essay.

location" as a way of identifying the person, the time, the place, and the culture that are mirrored in a particular theological perspective. Few of us assume anymore that one can describe the human condition of all persons the way Tillich attempted to do in volume 2 of his *Systematic Theology*. It is clear upon sustained reflection that the way Tillich poses the questions in his *Systematic Theology* carries with it the implied answers. (I realize that can be said of every theological system, but it is particularly clear in Tillich's thought.) Pluralism of course contains with it an acknowledgment of relativism. That once-dreaded word was defined by van Buren as being the view that "there is more than one way to look at any matter, and that what is said can be called true or false only in the terms provided by the particular point of reference."[9] That viewpoint has certainly been widespread in aesthetics, modern physics, and literary theory, as well as in contemporary theology.

The point of this assessment is to recognize that quite apart from the work of Postmodernists, theologians themselves in the last twenty years have been acknowledging that we are moving into a new era. I am reminded of an old adage I first heard as a theological student, namely, "In theology the assumptions of one generation become the problems for the next."

III.

Let us turn now to Postmodernism as a shaping intellectual influence in our time.[10] Practically everyone who has sought to understand Post-

---

[9]Van Buren, "The Dissolution of the Absolute," 341.

[10]Good introductory works are Paul Lakeland, *Postmodernism* (Minneapolis: Fortress Press, 1997) and Maden Sarup, *An Introductory Guide to Poststructuralism and Postmodernism* (Athens GA: University of Georgia Press, 1989). Lakeland has keener theological interests than Sarup, however, Other valuable works include Jean-Francois Lyotard, *The Postmodern Condition* (Manchester, England: Manchester University Press, 1984), and the more critical view of British Marxist Terry Eagleton in *The Illusions of Postmodernism* (Cambridge: Blackwell Publishers, 1996). Eagleton objects to Postmodernism because he feels it has no sense of history and no interest in social change. Two shaping figures have been Jacques Derrida and Michel Foucault. On Derrida, see his *Of Grammatology* (Baltimore: Johns Hopkins University Press, 1976) and his *Writing and Difference* (Chicago: University of Chicago Press, 1978). On

modernism recognizes that it is a complex and amorphous phenomenon. It has many streams and nuances, as Paul Lakeland has noted. It has been interpreted in different ways, much like Existentialism in Europe at an earlier time in our century. In its literary form it has affinities with Post-structuralism, Romanticism, Comparative Linguistics, and Deconstruction theory. In its social and political form it has implications for aesthetics, architecture, ethics, and politics, as well as for religion and theology. It is always difficult to generalize about such a complex movement, but I think we can safely say that it is a movement that invites us to go beyond rationalism, beyond ontological assertions, and beyond literary and theological exclusiveness. It emphasizes pluralism, diversity, and the polymorphous nature of truth. Some have even maintained that the bottom line of Postmodernism is the protest of the marginalized against the cultural hegemony and power of ruling classes and institutions. Postmodernists have recognized that ideas have power; institutions have power; and literary and theological voices have privileged some people and experiences over others. Much depends on the power of a dominant group to set an agenda. For our purposes in this essay let us note several observations about the beginnings and growth of this movement.

1. Although Postmodernism has recently been pushing its way onto the theological agenda, its assumptions and critiques have been around for many years. Many philosophers link it to Kant; others to critical theory. It has roots in the work of the Swiss linguist Ferdinand de Saussure (1857–1913) who in the early days of the twentieth century wrote a series of essays exploring the relationship of language to reality.[11] Saussure argued that there is no transcendent reality beyond the symbolic function

---

Foucault, see his *Madness and Civilization* (London: Tavistock, 1967); *The Order of Things* (London: Tavistock, 1970); and *Power/Knowledge: Selected Interviews and Other Writings, 1972–1977*, ed. C. Gordon (Brighton, England: Harvestor Press, 1980). Both Derrida and Foucault have written other books and articles than these cited here.

[11]Saussure's major work, *Memoir on the Original System of Vowels in the Indo-European Languages*, published in 1879 while he was still a young man of 22, laid the foundation for the field of comparative linguistics. His work has been called "the starting point of twentieth-century linguistics." He was professor of Indo-European Linguistics and Sanskrit at the University of Geneva from 1891 to 1913.

of language. The more modern phase of Postmodernism is generally traced to October 1966, when a young (thirty-seven) French philosopher named Jacques Derrida presented a paper at a conference at Johns Hopkins University. He attacked the thought and assumptions of Claude Levi-Strauss, and in the process also attacked the Western tendency to assume a metaphysical structure in literary interpretations. The Johns Hopkins conference was on the theme of "The Languages of Criticism," so Derrida's initial work was oriented more toward literary critics. A big point for him was that there is no stable center to language. Language *per se* points to no ultimate reality or metaphysical truth. To recognize that need not be terrifying; it can instead be liberating, and allow us to sense the "play" in language.[12] Derrida has continued to be a major force in the evolution of the Postmodern movement. He feels that it brings liberation from oppressive social, political, and religious structures.

2. Postmodernism has had its major religious impact in textural studies, where amid discussions of hermeneutics and debates over methods of literary criticism scholars have been forced to deal with the views of Postmodernism. An important example in this debate is a book by the Bible and Culture Collective entitled *The Postmodern Bible*.[13] In the field of theological studies, there has been much more reluctance to engage the challenge of Postmodernism, because its claims are so threatening to theological structures and indeed to the churches themselves.[14]

---

[12]Derrida, "Structure, Sign, and Play in the Discourse of the Human Sciences," in *Writing and Difference*, 282-83.

[13]George Aichele et al., the Bible and Culture Collective (New Haven CT: Yale University Press, 1995). The *Postmodern Bible*, incidentally, includes only a single passing mention of Tillich, as one among several potential "godfathers" of "feminist essentialist theories or theologies of femininity" (265).

[14]There have been efforts, however, to address the issues raised. See Frederick Ferré *Shaping the Future: Resources for the Postmodern World* (New York: Harper & Row, 1976); David Ray Griffin, *God and Religion in the Postmodern World: Essays in Postmodern Theology*, Series in Constructive Postmodern Thought (New York: SUNY Press, 1989); and Roger Lundin, *The Culture of Interpretation: Christian Faith and the Postmodern World* (Grand Rapids MI: Eerdman's, 1993).

To date, three major conferences on "Religion and Postmodernism" have been held at Villanova University: (1) 25-27 September 1997; (2) 14-16 October

3. Scholars from many disciplines have added to the literature of Postmodernism. Practitioners of ideology criticism and feminist criticism have noted the issues of power and control in the interpretation of texts.[15] American philosopher Richard Rorty has argued in a pragmatic spirit that the truth for each person is what helps us to cope. He rejects therefore the claims of any eternal truth or metanarrative. For more than twenty years, the French philosopher Michel Foucault has contributed much to this movement; he has been particularly interested in the process of modernization, epistemology, the nature of the self, and how societies become homogenized internally.[16] The British philosopher Alasdair MacIntyre has criticized our middle-class value systems as "emotivism," and gives support to Postmodernist perspectives. Scholars in the field recognize affinities with the earlier thought of Friedrich Nietzsche, William James, Martin Heidegger, and Ralph Waldo Emerson. It is beyond the scope of this chapter to explore these links, but we need to note that this movement has been an interdisciplinary phenomenon, and sees itself as an extension of many nineteenth-century concerns.

From these broad observations, let us now sharpen our focus about Postmodernism and theological studies.

1999; and (3) 27-29 September 2001. Each of these conferences is characterized as an "international colloquium of philosophers and theologians devoted to the exploration of the questions of religion and interpretation at the end of the second millennium." Papers from the first two conferences have been published; papers from the third conference, "Confessions" (namely, a discussion of the relevance of Augustine's *Confessions*), will be published soon. The first two conference publications, both in the Indiana Series in the Philosophy of Religion, are as follows. *God, the Gift, and Postmodernism*, ed. John D. Caputo and Michael J. Scanlon (Bloomington: Indiana University Press, 1999) and *Questioning God*, ed. John D. Caputo, Mark Dooley, and Michael J. Scanlon (Bloomington: Indiana University Press, 2001).

[15]See *The Postmodern Bible* (New Haven CT: Yale University Press, 1995) chaps. 6 and 7.

[16]See the discussion of Foucault in Sarup, *An Introductory Guide to Poststructuralism and Postmodernism*, 63-95; and in Paul Lakeland's *Postmodernism*.

(1) Postmodernism stresses the contextual nature of all thought. All literary interpretations and theological interpretations are therefore relative to place, personhood, and culture.

(2) In response to people who make absolute statements or claims for their literary or theological interpretations, Postmodernism insists that there is no self-evident single interpretation of scriptures, literary texts, ethical assertions, or dogmatic statements. This is of course very threatening to most religious traditions, which assert to their followers that they have an accurate "map of the world" and are transmitting God's plan for human belief and action. Postmodernists recognize that we still have to make personal judgments between relative claims, but these are judgments based on our experience in the context of our own search for meaning. Ethical, literary, and aesthetic judgments are matters of personal preference, and there is no conclusive way to verify our value preferences to the satisfaction of others.

(3) It follows that claims for the existence of an "Absolute" are no longer needed or helpful. We do not need to ground our epistemology in a theory of an Absolute. We have no need for metaphysical language, and no need to press our religious claims into some holistic vision of the world. Everyone's viewpoint contains some truth and merit.

Setting itself directly against the assumptions of the so-called modern or Enlightenment period, Postmodernism maintains that reality is undecidable and the world is *no particular way* at all. It is now clear that older thought systems were expressed through political ideologies that extended privilege to white, established males, and that aesthetic, literary, and theological opinions are in fact simply culturally conditional statements of personal judgment. "Holy Toledo!" says the Tillich scholar. "What sense can I make of this?"

IV.

Perhaps the first instinct of Tillich scholars is to fold our tents and silently steal away. It seems the assumptions of Postmodernist thought are so diametrically opposed to Tillich's way of thinking that there is no middle ground. There are some areas, however, where Tillich scholars and Postmodernists have common concerns. Both criticize misleading dogmatic pronouncements that are associated with religious traditions. Both expose the arrogance with which some groups claim that they know the will of God. Both agree that religious groups mirror the ethos of their

geographical region and middle-class constituencies. Both acknowledge
the privileging of white males in our society, and the privileging of some
people's experience and thoughts over others. Insofar as Postmodernism
exposes the biases and assumptions that have shaped our intellectual,
political, and social life, it has value for those who continue to work in
a Tillichian spirit.

This is not to say, however, that there is an easy blending between
Tillich's worldview and that of the Postmodernists. Major gaps divide
these two ways of understanding reality. If we were to grant most of the
assumptions of Postmodernism, could we still lead religious lives? Or is
Postmodernism the demise of the Christian religion as we have known it
and proclaimed it? I see five ways—there may be more—for Christian
theology to respond to Postmodernism.

(1) Basing our stance on the method and assumptions of Karl Barth,
we can ignore the whole movement. Such a stance of course would rest
on a high view of biblical authority and on special interpretations of
revelation and epistemology. In this position we could declare that
literary theory and philosophy have nothing to do with the work of
Christian theology. We could say that it is "of the world," and hence of
no interest or significance for those who trust God's revelation in the
Bible and who seek to live out biblical faith. Barth, it will be remembered, summarily dismissed historical criticism, dialectics with
philosophy, and studies in religion and culture. In one way or other, this
seems to me to be the response of most seminaries I know. Whatever
else they teach, they do not teach about Postmodernism. (They do not
teach much about Freud, Marx, Nietzsche, Eliade, or Joseph Campbell,
either.) I will leave it to my readers to evaluate whether this Barthian
position would be a viable response in our time.

(2) A second response might reclaim the theological posture of
William Hamilton, who was so prominent in the "Death of God" movement in the 1960s. Hamilton basically declared that the image or vision
of the biblical God that has sustained Christianity for more than 1900
years is gone; that modern persons no longer have need of the God hypothesis; and that the task is to live a creative and meaningful life based
on the model and memory of Jesus. Writing in 1964, Hamilton claimed
that today's theologian has neither faith nor hope, but only love as a
guide. Postmodernists share a lot of that worldview and in fact speak of
the "Protean Person" as a model. There are of course some affinities
with the existentialist movement of an earlier generation implicit in the

Postmodernist vision: we can no longer trust or assume that there is some supreme power or entity that is directing the world and imbuing it with meaning. In some ways we are each on our own, shaped by families and communities and professional interests as we try to deconstruct the hidden meanings behind our legal, political, and intellectual lives. Here religion is basically ethical and not metaphysical.[17]

(3) A third response might take us back to more careful language analysis, similar to the perspectives of A. J. Ayer, Frederick Ferré, Ian Ramsey, and of course Ludwig Wittgenstein. Wittgenstein's observations about "language games" would refocus our concerns to what language is and how it functions; metaphysical speculations give way to the mystery of language and its contextual use. This brings more modesty to our theological assertions and would recast what we feel we can say about the Christian tradition, but it is a way to respond seriously to the changing intellectual climate. This type of work is safe and academically responsible. Whether this position gives us much of a life vision is another matter.

(4) A fourth possible response would be to follow the lead of David Griffin. In his provocative book *God and Religion in the Postmodern World* (1989),[18] Griffin reminds us that there is both a negative and positive side to Postmodernism. The negative is stripping away our belief in the institutions and hierarchies of the modern era. The positive side is what he calls a "naturalistic theism" or "theistic naturalism." This gives us an openness to the future, an appreciation of the natural world, an openness to change. Although his model sounds like a revised interpretation of process theology, he does not think that Postmodernism necessarily strips us of faith or hope. It can be a tool, he argues, for us to understand our identity and to find meaning in a complex and ever changing world.

(5) Of course we could move beyond any claims for Christian exclusivism and ally ourselves with world religion studies and cross-cultural studies. Various thinkers offer clues about this: Joseph Campbell, Huston Smith, Mircea Eliade, Ninian Smart, and Wilfred Cantwell Smith, to name but a few. Campbell's thesis that religion is

---

[17]See Hamilton's *The New Essence of Christianity* (Philadelphia: Westminster, 1966) and his articles "Thursday's Child" and "The Death of God Theologies Today" in William Hamilton and Thomas Altizer, *Radical Theology and the Death of God* (Indianapolis: Bobbs-Merrill, 1968) 87-94 and 23-52.

[18]See n. 14 above.

ultimately about life's journey, and that religious texts and rituals enhance that journey, is a viewpoint consistent with Postmodernism. This method removes the absolutism and exclusiveness from Christianity, and allows for diversity and personal truth. Christianity is seen as one historical symbol system among the many.

Most Postmodernists urge us to accept a plurality of viewpoints when we think about life and the world. If we take Postmodernism seriously, our own theological statements will be more modest and tentative. We will recognize that there are more voices and experiences than we have been willing to consider in theological discourse. Out of a simple concern for fairness, we might be moved to support the voices of disadvantaged or pressed peoples. We will see through the ideologies of Euro-American culture. We may say less about "Truth" and more about "meaning." We might pay more attention to the findings of social scientists who ask about the self and its communities rather than to offer theological pronouncements about how God acts in history. Postmodernism recasts the theological agenda in substance and in style.

V.

Let us now sum up these reflections. Are there any absolutes left? The answer depends on whom we listen to, what we take to be authoritative, how we envision "faith," and how we interpret the relationship of religion and culture. But one thing seems to be true: the metanarratives are gone. Although Postmodernist thought has provoked much criticism, what is troubling for some theologians is how much truth there is in its various observations. Although I once thought (with Tillich) that theology could be done from a more-or-less neutral perspective that could illumine our plight as human beings, I now believe that all theological work is contextual and limited. We might be able to talk about our personal absolutes even when we can no longer presume an ultimate Absolute. Tillich, however, does provide a corrective to the power of Postmodernist thought. He recognized that human beings live by faith, trust, passions, and symbols. Even if these are not empirically proveable they have power to shape life and destiny. Such visions do become personal absolutes and most people need something like that to live a purposeful life.

A Tillich scholar can recognize that there is truth in the overall view of Postmodernism but need not feel intimidated or negated by it. My studies in comparative religious have helped me see in retrospect that pluralism is not a bad thing; that relativism is not a bad thing; that modesty in theological claims is not a bad thing; that ideology criticism is not a bad thing. Courage, honesty, openness, and compassion are constructive things and we can try to incorporate those virtues even without a sense that our values or lifestyles should be models for all people. Even within a more modest conceptual framework, we can affirm the reality of grace and of a healing Spirit. And Tillich, who has been such a mentor for us, can be appreciated for his vision and encyclopedic interests, but we can see him more clearly as a product of his time and his cultures. His time, unfortunately, is no longer our time. But as he always has, he still gives us a beacon in time of confusion and courage amid uncertainty. We can be glad for that.

Chapter 9

PUBLIC AND PRIVATE ETHICS: REFLECTIONS ON TILLICH'S LIFE AND ETHICAL THEORY

The ethical element is a necessary—and often predominant—element in every theological statement. —Paul Tillich, *Systematic Theology* 1:31

With the Bill Clinton-Monica Lewinsky debacle in 1998–1999, America was once again confronted with the issue of public versus private ethics. Even feminists who had been supportive of Bill Clinton's political priorities were puzzled as to how to respond to his personal behavior, and wondered about his future political credibility. Do personal faults and shortcomings destroy a political leader's credibility? Given the fact that Bill Clinton was a head of state, apparently lied under oath, and suffered the embarrassment of an impeachment trial, why should anyone trust his word in the future? We have seen such perplexities raised previously in American political life, but the Clinton scandal brought the conflict between the personal and public areas of life once again onto center stage.

This is of interest to Tillich scholars because it again brings into consciousness the allegations made against Paul Tillich by his wife Hannah in her book *From Time to Time*, published in 1973.[1] The controversy created by her book and a counterpoint book by Rollo May entitled *Paulus*—also published in 1973 as an apparent attempt to blunt the bitter comments of Hannah Tillich[2]—led to an extended debate on the relationship of Tillich's life to his thought. That debate was extended and somewhat exacerbated by Wilhelm Pauck and Marion Pauck in their 1976

---

[1](New York: Stein and Day, 1973).

[2]The subtitle variations may be noteworthy: *Paulus: Reminiscences of a Friendship* (New York: Harper & Row, 1973); *Paulus: A Personal Portrait of Paul Tillich* (New York: Harper & Row, 1973); *Paulus: Tillich as Spiritual Teacher*, rev. ed. (Dallas TX: Saybrook, 1987, 1988).

offering, *Paul Tillich: His Life and Thought*.[3] We do not have to reopen that debate here, since it generated a great deal of discussion and in fact I contributed two articles on the topic myself.[4] (The German response to that debate is discussed in appendix B, below.)

In the past few years, however, three scholars have reappraised those issues and have reopened the discussion about Tillich's ethics and personal credibility. One is Alexander Irwin, whose views and my response to them are discussed above in chapter 6. A second volume came from Grace Cali, Tillich's secretary during his Harvard years (1956–1962): *Paul Tillich Firsthand*.[5] Cali does not address the Hannah Tillich allegations directly but does describe some conversations she had with Tillich about marriage and other relationships. The third essay was from a young American feminist, Tracy Fessenden, in her article "Woman and the 'Primitive' in Paul Tillich's Life and Thought: Some Implications for the Study of Religion."[6]

It is my primary goal in this chapter to review and appraise Tillich's ethical theory, but any effort to do that has to acknowledge the tension between Tillich's private life and his public ethical theory. Let us first look at the themes and arguments in the work of Cali and Fessenden, and see what new, if anything, they have contributed to this debate that has been with us for more than a quarter of a century.

---

[3]Vol. 1, *Life* (New York: Harper & Row, 1976).

[4]Some of the representative literature would include Tom Driver, "Scandalous Existence," *New Republic* (24 November 1973): esp. p. 28; Melvin Vulgamore, "Tillich's Erotic Solution", *Encounter* 45/3 (Summer 1984): 193-212; Ann B. Ulanov, "Between Anxiety and Faith: The Role of the Feminine in Tillich's Theological Thought," in *Paul Tillich on Creativity*, ed. Jacquelyn Ann E. Kegley (Landham MD: University Press of America, 1989) esp. 140-42; Donald McKinnon, *Explorations in Theology 5* (London: SCM Press, 1979) 130-34; and Seward Hiltner, "Tillich the Person," in *Theology Today* 30/4 (January 1974): 382-88. My contributions were "Morality and Beyond: Tillich's Ethics in Life and in Death," in *Tillich Studies: 1975*, ed. John J. Carey (Tallahassee FL: The North American Paul Tillich Society, 1975) 104-13; and "Life on the Boundary: The Paradoxical models of Tillich and Pike," in *The Duke Divinity School Review* 42/3 (Fall 1977): 149-64.

[5]Subtitled *A Memoir of the Harvard Years*, intro. by Jerald C. Brauer (Chicago: Exploration Press, 1996).

[6]In *Journal of Feminist Thought in Religion* 14/20 (Fall 1998): 45-76.

I.

Grace Cali's book is not intended to shed new light on Tillich's ethics as much as it gives us a glimpse into his work habits, letters, travels, friendships, and conversations during his Harvard years. In chapter 2 of her book, however, she does recount some conversations she had with Tillich in 1957 about love, marriage, and the "bourgeois mentality" which Tillich thought most Americans had about marriage. Cali, who tended to record in her private journal conversations she had had with Tillich, recounts that he felt that marriage, by its very nature, eventually and naturally excludes romance. Tillich felt, however, that romance (that is, Eros) is an essential ingredient of human creativity. Tillich refused to accept the prevailing American philosophy of marriage "with its cold, legalistic restrictions." Europeans, he felt, were much more realistic and flexible in their understanding of marriage. The only solution, he maintained, was a permissive attitude towards some limited romantic attachments outside of marriage. This, he maintained, does not necessarily lead to promiscuity or irresponsibility, but to a thoughtful openness to a limited number of persons. From our perspective today it seems clear that Tillich favored a limited form of "open" marriage, but felt that his public image as a married man was essential for his professional statues. Cali's book, in truth, does not break any new ground concerning Tillich's views on marriage beyond what the Paucks had already reported, but she does seem to support Rollo May's perspective on Tillich more than the view of Hannah Tillich.

Of course Tillich was not the first or only person to quarrel with the prevailing model of marriage in America. Much academic work on this has been done by sociologists, family therapists, and scholars in the field of Home and Family Studies. Feminists have critiqued marriage as an unhealthy institution for women, primarily on the grounds that traditional models usually make women subordinate. Marriage as an institution has been repudiated by many young people who cohabit, by elderly couples in retirement communities who do not want the legal or financial restrictions that our society attaches to marriage, and by gay couples. Our high divorce rate symbolizes the dissatisfaction so many people have with marriage. Marriage and family therapists have pretty much rejected the view that there is one normative model of marriage, and have concluded that a good marriage is what works for the two people involved. Hannah

Tillich's criticism, of course, was that Paulus wanted to understand their marriage in an open way, but she did not. (The paradox is that Hannah's book made it clear that she also had multiple relationships, so their marriage is a hard one for outsiders to understand.) Much of Tillich's thought about marriage is related to his positive sense of Eros, as Irwin has shown.

More substantial light is shed on Tillich's life and thought by Tracy Fessenden. She essentially takes at face value what Hannah Tillich says about Paulus: that he was unfaithful; that he followed a Bohemian life style in Europe; and that he was intrigued by women all of his adult life. Fessenden sees Tillich as a sexually driven man, and feels there was a great divide between Tillich's personal life and his professional persona. What is interesting, however, is her research into Tillich's early writings that show his fascination with primitive life and art forms: statues, dance masks, crafts, and fetishes. For Tillich, primitive cultures recognized elements of the irrational, the exotic, the unpredictable, and the subconscious, all of which express the depths of reality. Fessenden cites Tillich's famous 1926 article on the Demonic,[7] which claims that "Negro sculpture" and Shiva pictures, as they depict breasts, thighs, and sex organs, are pointing to organs of the will to power. They symbolize that there is such a things as "orgiastic ecstasy," domains of life far beyond the rational and ordinary. There are dimensions of life that are dark, mysterious, savage, exotic, and energizing. These, Tillich felt, must have their parallels with the Divine Life. This fascination with the primitive, Fessenden maintains, helps us understand Tillich's fascination with the Expressionist movement in art, as well as his interest in black erotic power that he sensed in his visits to Harlem with Hannah.

More significantly for our purposes here, Fessenden argues that Tillich understood the female gender as embodying this deeper, mysteri-

---

[7]"Der Begriff des Dämonischen und seine Bedeutung für die systematische Theologie" (Tübingen, 1926). (A typescript, item 204:061, is archived in the Tillich Archives at Harvard.) A later article (1929), "Das Dämonische, ein Beitrag zur Sinndeutung der Geshcichte," was translated as "The Demonic" and published as chap. 1 of part 2 ("Philosophical Categories of the Interpretation of History") of Tillich's *The Interpretation of History*, trans. Nicholas Alfred Rasetzki (part 1) and Elsa L. Talmey (parts 2, 3, and 4) (New York and London: Charles Scribner's Sons, 1936).

ous, powerful stream of life. Hence, Fessenden maintains, Tillich was drawn to women with an intuitive sense that they would understand him and his system. They are bearers of joy, danger, and pleasure. They have "powers of origin." It follows that for Tillich relationships with women have the potential for "reunion" and wholeness that he wrote so much about in his more general ethical theory. His interest in women needs to be understood, therefore, not so much as a "wandering eye" of a lustful man, but in a theological or psychological sense. (We should note in passing, however, that there are other nuances in Tillich's thought about the Demonic beyond what Fessenden considers in her article.[8])

There are other aspects of Fessenden's article, particularly her lament about Tillich's influence on the study of religion, which are important, but her main contribution for our purposes is her attribution that Tillich's interest in women was a deeper, intuitive sense of women as bearers of mysterious powers of reality. Like Irwin, Fessenden sees a great influence of Freud on Tillich, especially Freud's view of the human psyche. On the whole, she does not think that in life or in thought Tillich offers the contemporary Christian world a good model for ethics.

The modern interpreter of Tillich needs to reflect on Fessenden's arguments. Was Tillich's interest in the primitive a major influence on his ethical thought? Is it a clue to his personal life and ethical theory? Or were there other aspects of his experience that we also need to recognize as we try to understand his pilgrimage of thought? I would say we need to temper Fessenden's argument with the recognition that Tillich's experience as a military chaplain in the First World War, his experience of economic and social chaos during the waning days of the Weimar Republic, his struggle against fascism, his experience of crossing the ocean at age forty-seven, and his visit to Japan in 1960 were all profound experiences in his life and thought. His interest in primitive cultures helps us understand some features of this multifaceted thinker, but surely not all. Was he right in his sense of the mystery of women, or was he (even unknowingly) perpetuating an ideology about women that feminists today find painful? Was he himself enmeshed in an ideology of his time and

---

[8]See, e.g., the article by H. Frederick Reise, Jr., "The Demonic as a Principle in Tillich's Doctrine of God," in *Theonomy and Autonomy: Studies in Paul Tillich's Engagement with Modern Culture*, ed. John J. Carey (Macon GA: Mercer University Press, 1984) 135-56.

culture about women that he could not see through? Did his understanding of women lead him to cultivate women as personal followers of his?
There are serious questions, and must be kept in mind as we assess his
ethical theory. Yet as we proceed we must also keep in mind that there
are other dimensions of this man that we must understand if we are to
grasp his broader approach to ethics. It is to that broader task that we
now turn.

II.

Four preliminary things need to be said before we turn to Tillich's
ethical theory. The first is that it was long an axiom among Tillich
scholars that Tillich's contribution to twentieth-century religious thought
was in systematic theology and studies in religion and culture. We tried
to dispel that myth in *Being and Doing: Paul Tillich as Ethicist.*[9] Even
so, it is true that Tillich tended to approach ethical issues from a
philosophical and theoretical perspective, and offered few concrete
examples when he was writing about ethics. Grace Cali reports that she
chided Tillich about that, but he replied that if the theory is understood,
its implications for concrete situations would be readily understandable.
He feared that too many concrete examples would be taken as offering
easy answers to complex problems. Yet his interest in life's ethical
quandaries was wide and genuine, and all of his professional life he
struggled with major ethical issues.

A second observation is that the field of ethics has changed and split
into many subcategories since Tillich's time. The influence of feminists,
black theologians, and third world thinkers has made it clear that we
cannot assume any longer that there is just one way of reading the human
condition, or even one self-evident starting place for ethical reflection.
The field has become more specialized: we now read about business
ethics, ecological concerns, feminist ethics, medical ethics, ethics and
public policy (for example, health care, abortion rights, capital punish-
ment, urban problems, and so forth), ethics of other religious traditions
(generally called comparative-religion ethics), animal rights, and sexual
ethics, to name but a few important subfields.

---

[9]Ed. John J. Carey (Macon GA: Mercer University Press, 1987).

Tillich's interests have to be seen as broadly generalized, as dealing with the struggle to find meaning and purpose in life. His ethical writing has to be seen in relation to his dominant theological theme that the great Divine work is bringing humanity from broken, finite Being to restored and whole Being. Tillich thought his ethical guidelines would be helpful to all persons as they struggle with human limitations and brokenness. Whether or not we can assume that is a major issue in evaluating the continuing helpfulness of his ethical thought. (Chapter 5 above considers that issue with regard to Tillich's *The Courage to Be*.)

A third observation is a reminder that the field of ethics traditionally has been divided into social ethics and personal ethics, or public ethics and private ethics. Social ethics has dealt with issues of life in community: what guidelines, policies, and attitudes are most beneficial in creating a fair and just society? Not surprisingly, such reflections usually lead to political analysis and to political advocacy. As we noted in chapter 3, Tillich was most active in this arena during his German years while enmeshed in the struggles of the Weimar Republic. In those days he wrote a great deal about class struggles and justice. His views mirrored a socialist perspective and reflected a sharp criticism of capitalism. Since we have looked at these themes in chapters 2 and 3, our concentration in this chapter will be on his writings about personal ethics—the search for a purposive life. These writings come from his American period, and are where we see the closest interaction of his life and thought.

The fourth preliminary observation is that the field of ethics can easily become abstract and academic, and make little sense to the person who is hurting and wants some direction about how to make sense out of a perplexed life. Tillich contributes his share of abstraction in his ethical writings, to be sure, but I will endeavor in this chapter to describe his views with as much clarity as I can. His sermons are sharper and more lucid, for example, than his *Systematic Theology*, and many of his lectures are easier to follow than his philosophical writings such as *Love, Power, and Justice*.[10] The one book that Tillich authored that dealt

---

[10]Tillich, *Love, Power, and Justice: Ontological Analyses and Ethical Applications*, Firth Lectures in Nottingham, England; Sprunt Lectures in Richmond, Virginia (New York: Oxford University Press, 1953).

exclusively with ethics and morality was *Morality and Beyond*,[11] and it remains a primary source, particularly the final chapter entitled "Ethics in a Changing World." Broadly speaking, in terms of today's viewpoints in Christian ethics, Tillich has more in common with some aspects of feminist theory, situation ethics, and liberation ethicists than with divine-command ethics, natural-law theorists, or with legalists of any stripe. For Tillich no static approach to law or morality will do. All ethical theory must take into account the fluidity of life and ever-changing human situations. In *Morality and Beyond* he noted that "Change, being the chief character of life, is also the chief character of ethics" (85).

III.

Tillich's approach to ethics perhaps may best be classified as a self-realization ethic. He felt that the Divine wills for each of us the actualization of our potential, as divine Grace moves us from finite Being to essential (that is, "whole") being. In *Morality and Beyond* he suggested that "The moral imperative is the demand to become actually what one is essentially and therefore potentially" (20). In his *Systematic Theology* he wrote:

> Thus, within the process of actualization of the potential, which is called life, we distinguish the three functions of life: self-integration under the principle of centeredness, self-creation under the principle of growth, and self-transcendence under the principle of sublimity. (*ST* 3:31-32)

This self-actualization, however, becomes a reality only through the power of Agape love and the concrete reality of each moment, which Tillich liked to call the "Kairos." (Kairos is a powerful theme in Tillich's thought, and full exploration of it is beyond our purposes here. In this context of ethical theory, Tillich is using it just to refer to concrete times and circumstances.) It is for this reason that I would call Tillich a "situation" ethicist, to refer to a viewpoint that Joseph Fletcher and John

---

[11]Religious Perspectives 9 (New York: Harper & Row, 1963); most recently in the Library of Theological Ethics series, foreword by William Schweiker (Louisville: Westminster/John Knox Press, 1995).

A. T. Robinson made famous in ethical theory.[12] We are not simply left on our own, however, to decide as best we can in each changing circumstance, as some humanists and existentialists have maintained. Broadly speaking, Tillich felt that the human quest for purposive life is guided by the great principles of Agape, Justice, and Wisdom, all applied to specific contexts. Even these guiding principles, however, are not static, but are always in the process of change and reinterpretation. Let us now consider how these three principles intertwine.

IV.

Love, Tillich argues, is the only reality that has two sides that seem to be contradictory: completely united on the one hand, it is unconditional; on the other hand, it is more flexible than any other spiritual reality. It is the one power in us that is able to adapt itself to every kind of unique situation. It enables us to listen to what the other really wants and may not be able to say, or to sense what he or she might be lacking without knowing it. *Agape* is what binds us responsibly to other persons, as well as to ourselves and to our world as a whole. Tillich argues that "love liberates us from the bondage to absolute ethical traditions, to conventional morals and to authorities that claim to know the right decisions perhaps without having listened to the demands of the unique moment."[13] Love breaks the prison of any absolute moral laws even when they are vested with the authority of sacred traditions.

For Tillich the ethical quest is to find centeredness, meaning, and purpose amid the ambiguities of life. In *Love, Power, and Justice* Tillich attempted to show how these three dimensions of life and personhood have an ontological grounding. In *Morality and Beyond* he attempted to show how justice and love are related to human experience. Our sense of justice, he maintained, is rooted in our encounters with other persons: in our recognition that other persons participate in the divine life and have unlimited potential. It is appropriate, therefore, to treat such persons as

---

[12]Their now-classic opening salvos of course were John Arthur Thomas Robinson, *Honest to God* (London: SCM Press; Philadelphia: Westminster Press, 1963) and Joseph F. Fletcher, *Situation Ethics: The New Morality* (London: SCM Press; Philadelphia: Westminster Press, 1966).

[13]*Morality and Beyond*, 43.

a "Thou." That recognition extends to *all* human beings, regardless of sex, caste, or social rank; this concern for fairness and equality can be called justice. It is important to note that justice for Tillich as an ethical principle is not primarily legal and impersonal; it is derived from the fundamental experience of a person-to-person encounter.

Justice, however, must be yoked with *agape* love as a means of enabling selves to come together. Tillich writes, "If love is the ultimate norm of all moral demands, its' *agape* quality points to the transcendent source of the content of the moral imperative. For *agape* transcends the finite possibility of man."[14] *Agape* is both life and world affirming. It stands against asceticism and human detachment.

Tillich's third principle of ethics is wisdom, which he defines as the cumulation of laws and conventions of many religions and cultures. Wisdom is distilled, not simply from earlier revelations, but also from human experience, and, as such, conventional codes of morality can be regarded as being for the most part valid. They are "guides" to help us assess possibilities for action in any given situation. Such wisdom, however, must not be followed unconditionally. Coming to personhood requires a willingness to take risks in ethical decision making. In a 1962 lecture, Tillich noted:

Nobody can be a person who doesn't risk in his or her ethical decisions. Those who did it—who broke through—were the most lonely people, and if you, any of you, want to break through the values of this wisdom of mankind, you might be right. You risk much and you will be lonely, but perhaps if you do so you will have become a person, and if you do not do so, you may have missed your own fulfillment as a person. This is the dimension in which our ethical situation stands."[15]

In sum, morality for Tillich deals with self-realization. Moral acts are those in which we actualize our potentiality as persons. We come to moments of decision making guided by respect for others and the wisdom of the past, but always open to the unique opportunities of each moment.

---

[14]*Morality and Beyond*, 40.

[15]"Ethical Principles of Moral Action," a lecture given at Florida State University, March 2, 1962, and published in *Being and Doing: Paul Tillich as Ethicist*, ed. John J. Carey (Macon GA: Mercer University Press, 1987) 205-17; the passage cited is on p. 217 and the emphasis (italics) is in the original.

For those who would come to maturity, some risks are essential, for life is a venture to be lived rather than a problem to be defined.

I have felt for many years that the fruit of Tillich's ethics is best discerned in his sermons. I have asked myself time and again why his sermons are so powerful, and why I, along with countless other persons, still turn to them for inspiration and insight. The basic answer, I believe, is that in his sermons Tillich takes seriously the dark side of human nature. Informed by death psychology and existentialist analysis, he deals with problems of human sin and guilt, and of fear and anxiety, brokenness and healing. He probes the differences between what society asks us to do and be and what in fact we are. He rejects those "men of good will" who tell us to be good,[16] and condemns those who in pulpit, schools, or family call the natural sexual strivings of the body sinful. In his sermon "Do Not Be Conformed" he argues that only those who are prepared to take risks can renew their own being and thus renew other beings.[17] The person open to the spirit has to resist making ultimates of our world, our culture, our churches, or our moral codes, and those who never risk, and who therefore never fail, are those who are the true failures in life.

In ways we have not understood before, the various studies of Tillich's life illumine why Tillich chose to preach on a number of the texts that he did. It is not accidental that he preached on Paul's famous text in Romans 7, "The Good That I Will, I Do Not," and why he addressed himself to such topics as conformity, the demonic, being forgiven, and accepting our own acceptance. It now seems clear that Tillich struggled profoundly in his own life with the problem of guilt and alienation. Despite his professional prominence he knew the problem of loneliness and despair. He could preach as he did because of a need to make sense of his own life, to cope with his own fears and dark side, and to explain his own rejection of conventional morality.

SOME ASSESSMENTS

Agape love, justice, wisdom, risk, all experienced within changing Kairoi—are these themes solid enough to serve as the foundation of a

---

[16]*The Eternal Now*, 43.
[17]*The Eternal Now*, 139-40.

Christian ethic? They are general, to be sure, and perhaps ambiguous, but they reflect Tillich's view that life is dynamic and is ever opening up to new circumstances. For Tillich, in fact, all of life is ambiguous, and maturity is tested by how well we deal with ambiguity. Tillich had some sympathy with Whitehead's view that life is an adventure, and he was mindful that cultures and institutions have tendencies to establish laws and moral codes. Social laws and customs may have accrued wisdom on their side, but they serve us best as guides and not as masters. In this sense Tillich stands with Fletcher and Robinson in his insistence that agape love is above the laws that serve those institutions and cultures. (Martin Luther King's protest against segregation laws would be an example of this, as would Gandhi's protest against various British laws in India.) There are no divine commands in Tillich's ethical theory, and no easy answers for the multiple dilemmas each human being has to face. Risks abound, and uncertainty will be an ever-present factor. This is not an ethic for the timid or insecure. For those, however, who find themselves propelled out of the old securities and into the uncharted waters of life, Tillich still offers guidelines and something to hold unto.

There are blind spots in Tillich's ethical theory, however, which mirror the cultures and ethos of his lifetime. On the whole he was oblivious to the gender issues raised by subsequent feminist and womanist thinkers. He did not forsee the distinctive theological viewpoints of black theology or other ethnic traditions. He was not so sensitive to environmental/ecological issues, as we see in more recent thinkers like Sallie McFague or Matthew Fox. All of this means we cannot simply "reheat" Tillich's ethical thought and assume that it will speak to all of our contemporary problems. Some people simply cannot start where Tillich starts, and are distrustful of any ethic that is based so much on Spirit and Grace.

Perhaps the most pressing question, however, is whether the information about Tillich's lifestyle should negate his credibility as an ethicist or theologian. I think we can say that the biographical information we have about Paulus is sad and not deserving of emulation, but at the same time does not negate his broad ethical theory or his many rich theological insights. Information about the life quandaries of great composers does not detract from the power or beauty of their music. Biographical information about great poets or writers does not diminish the lasting significance of their work. Great contributions to intellectual life, culture, or political leadership do not require impeccable personal lives. Fessenden's penetrating article does not mean that we can or should psychologically dismiss Tillich's broader approach to ethics, nor does it mean that we should feel that Tillich's ethical theory was just self-serving for his own lifestyle. Tillich's ethical theory remains as one of a number of viable ways to think about a constructive and purposive life, and those who take the time to read his work still find him helpful.

There is the related question, of course, of whether or not Tillich's self-realization ethic can be called a Christian ethic. Initially it seems to have more in common with the approaches of humanistic psychologists such as Carl Rogers or Abraham Maslow. One looks in vain in Tillich's work on ethics for consideration of the themes of responsibility and covenant. As Seward Hiltner has pointed out, however, Tillich was never enamored of the institutional church, and may have felt that ethics of responsibility are too intertwined with class, convention, and institutional ideology.[18] Recent analyses of ideology, in fact, indicate that Tillich was years ahead of his time in refusing to yoke the Christian life with a predominantly middle-class, white-American morality. His stress on self-realization stands as a corrective to much of the self-denial emphasis that has pervaded Christian ethics; his approach to ethics surely has some affinities with recent liberation theologies.[19] At any rate, we are now sophisticated enough in approaches to ethics that we should not lightly dismiss Tillich's self-realization ethic as "unchristian." Here, as in so many other areas, Tillich emerges as a boundary thinker, probing the point of intersection of Christian and humanist concerns.

Tillich's life, I believe, can be seen as a lived parable about the human search for wisdom. His own words are an appropriate epitaph:

> Wisdom loves the children of men, but she prefers those who come through foolishness to wisdom, and dislikes those who keep themselves equally distant from foolishness and from wisdom. They are the real fools, she would say, because they were never shaken by an encounter with the mystery of life, and therefore never able to see the unity of

---

[18]Hiltner, "Tillich the Person," 382-88.

[19]See Roger Shinn's comparison of Tillich and Gustavo Gutierrez in his essay, "Tension and Unity in the Ethics of Paul Tillich: An Exploration," in *Being and Doing*, ed. Carey, 26-27.

creation and destruction in the working of the divine wisdom. In those, however, who have recognized this working of wisdom, and become wise by it, artificial limits are broken down, often with great pain, and the real limits, the true measures are found. That is what happens when wisdom comes to men.[20]

---

[20]*The Eternal Now*, 169.

Appendix A

THE PAUL TILLICH ARCHIVES
AT HARVARD: A RESEARCH REPORT

There are two major archives that preserve Tillich's unpublished works, letters, personal mementos, and virtually all of his published works. These are located at the Andover-Harvard Theological Library at Harvard University and in the Special Collections Division of the library, and at the University of Marburg in Germany. I visited the Harvard archive in 1974 and again in 1993 while I was in residence at the university. The Paul Tillich Archives was established in 1967–1968 by Tillich's family and friends, and was subsequently expanded by the university with the help of an NEH grant. Its present space and holdings were established in 1985. In this essay, I will describe the Tillich materials that are available at Harvard, and comment on the organization of that material. The intent here is to give interested persons some sense of what the Harvard archive contains and how these materials can be utilized for research purposes.[1]

I.

The Tillich materials at Harvard are in two categories, the first and most notable of which include his unpublished lectures, class notes, dis-

---

[1][Editor's note.] See the author's report following his 1974 visit: John J. Carey, "Tillich Archives: A Bibliographical and Research Report," *Theology Today* 32/1 (April 1975): 46-55, in which he focuses on "(1) Tillich bibliography and corpus; (2) Tillich archives; and (3) Tillich societies." Carey's article is available online at <http://theologytoday.ptsem.edu/apr1975/v32-1-article4.htm>. The present report of course builds upon that earlier study, and is in part adapted here with the permission of the editors of *Theology Today*.

See now also the updated online inventory of the "Paul Tillich Archives" at the Andover-Harvard Theological Library—a complete listing and location index—at <http://oasis.harvard.edu/html/div00649.html>, which also includes administration information regarding access and use restrictions.

cussion transcripts, personal files, and assorted memorabilia and manuscripts.[2] This material is organized in the following manner.

Series A. Early German Notebooks, including the miscellaneous versions of Tillich's first two dissertations on Schilling, and notes on ethics, apologetics, dogmatics, Old Testament and New Testament, Hegel, art and religion, history of philosophy, and the history of Protestantism.

Series B. Tillich's early German published works, including lectures before 1933, theological writings, notes for seminars and courses (ethics, the interpretation of history, philosophy of religion, the present situation, doctrines of man, existentialism). Also here are letters, notes, addresses, comments, sermons, baptisms, and copies of Tillich's works translated from English.

Series C. Early unpublished notebooks in English (mostly Tillich's courses at Union Theological Seminary, New York, in the 1930s).

Series D. Unpublished English manuscripts.

Series E. Primarily of interest to editors and others who might wish to consult Tillich's handwritten first drafts of the following books: *The Courage to Be*; *Love, Power, and Justice: Biblical Religion and the Search for Ultimate Reality*; *Dynamics of Faith*; *Christianity and the Encounter of World Religions*; *Morality and Beyond*; and the three volumes of his *Systematic Theology*. This series also contains other miscellaneous published writings.

Series D, probably of most interest to Tillich scholars in America, covers a wide range of topics, and because of the interest and curiosity of those who have been influenced by Tillich, I will deal with these materials in some detail. For the most part, materials here are the handwritten notes of talks that Tillich gave to various groups and organizations, plus occasional, fully typed manuscripts of lectures that he gave at various universities. In some instances, both the original handwritten notes and a typed version are available in the same folio. Frequently, the notes for talks are merely condensed and simplified versions of topics that Tillich had previously explored in print; various talks on existentialism, Protestantism, and religious socialism would be cases in point. There are several typed transcriptions of radio programs and interviews which

---

[2]A much-dated but still helpful early description of material in the Harvard archives appeared in the *Harvard Divinity Bulletin* n.s. 1/2 (Winter 1968): 14-16.

Tillich granted; the range of subject matter is interesting ("The Theological Significance of Schweitzer," with Gerald Brauer in 1959; a roundtable discussion on philosophy with Charles Hartshorne, Walter Kaufmann, Helmut Thielicke, J. H. Randall, and others in 1959; "Theories and Problems of Aging," at Santa Barbara in 1965). The style is informal, and it seems clear Tillich did not intend this material for publication.

There are some fascinating personal impressions of Tillich's travels. He wrote a lengthy report to his friends of his visit to Japan in 1960, after he returned to Cambridge, and a similar account of his impressions of Israel, after his trip there in 1963. (The latter report was written from Chicago in 1964.)

For scholarly purposes, however, there are three areas in which unpublished manuscripts can extend our present knowledge of Tillich's thought: (1) in ethics, (2) Judaism, and (3) in the interaction between theology and psychology.

(1) *Ethics.* The Harvard archives contain lectures Tillich gave on "Religion and Sex," "The Development of Personal Morality," "Sex Relations, Love, and Marriage," "The Christian Message and the Moral Law," and "Ground for Moral Choice in a Pluralistic Society." (This last lecture, given by Tillich in a slightly different form at three universities in 1964, has been flagged by the Tillich estate.) It seems clear that in his approach to ethics, Tillich was exploring the boundary lines between the Judeo-Christian tradition and liberal humanism. He recognized the tensions posed by these alternative perspectives but felt that it was necessary to preserve the vitality of humanism. Seeking alternatives to the norms of "love" or "responsibility" so long associated with Christian ethics, Tillich poses the question: "What is the depth of our own particular kind of humanity?" The issue is whether or not we can say "yes" to our humanity, and can live with the risks and courage this requires. Tillich seemed to be grappling for an alternative to the "divine-command" approach to ethics and clearly was attracted to aspects of a self-realization ethic. Tillich stressed that in this borderline living we are not just isolated individuals but are sustained by a latent spiritual community that exists in a pluralistic society. In almost all of his lectures on ethics, Tillich emphasized the need for both fresh answers and fresh questions about the meaning of the good life. His deepest concern was that people will tire of the intensity of a new search for meaning and will lapse into the traditional models of thought and value. Earlier than most Western theolo-

gians, he sensed that the old absolutes were crumbling and that creative life requires both courage and the capacity to live with ambiguity.

(2) *Judaism.* Tillich had a long-standing interest in the Jewish people and in Judaism as a faith. Perhaps the fullest statement of his concern is found in his four Berlin lectures, delivered in 1953, on "Die Judenfrage, ein christliches und ein deutsches Problem."[3] There are four manuscripts that show Tillich's special concern for Judaism and Germany: "Can the Jew return to Germany?" (a handwritten manuscript of a talk given in 1946); "The Religious Relation between Christianity and Judaism in the Future" (typescript, no date); "Protestantism and Anti-Semitism" (typescript, no date), and "My Changing Thought on Zionism" (a revised but unpublished typescript of a talk Tillich gave in Chicago in 1959; restricted by the Tillich estate).

Tillich made an important distinction between anti-Semitism and anti-Judaism; he felt that much of Lutheran and other conservative Protestant resentment against the Jews was in the theological resistance of the Jews to the universal claim of the gospel. As long as Christians assert that individual salvation is dependent on faith in Jesus as the Christ there will be tension with Jews. This tension can be called "anti-Judaism." Yet "anti-

---

[3]*Die Judenfrage, ein christliches und ein deutsches Problem; view Vorträge, gehalten an der Deutschen Hochschule für Politik,* Schriftenreihe der Deutschen Hochschule für Politik Berlin (Berlin: Gebr. Weiss, 1953) 48 pp. These lectures are analyzed in detail by Glenn D. Earley in his article "Paul Tillich and Judaism: An Analysis of 'The Jewish Question—A Christian and a German Problem,' " in *Theonomy and Autonomy,* ed. John J. Carey (Macon GA: Mercer University Press, 1984) 213-37. Lectures 2 and 4 were translated as "The Jewish Question: Christian and German Problem," in *Jewish Social Studies* 33/4 (October 1971): 253-71, and an offprint was published by the Conference on Jewish Social Studies in New York (1971). Apparently the only complete English translation of the lectures remains that of Earley in his dissertation: "An Everlasting Conversation: Judaism in the Theology of Paul Tillich" (Temple University, 1984).

Tillich's first Voice of America radio address into occupied Europe during World War II (he delivered 112 such addresses, March 1942–May 1944) was on "The Jewish Question," and this address appears in translation in *Against the Third Reich: Paul Tillich's Wartime Addresses to Nazi Germany,* trans. Matthew Lon Weaver, ed. Ronald H. Stone and Matthew Lon Weaver (Louisville; Westminster/John Knox Press, 1998).

Semitism" is a different thing. It speaks of Jewish inferiority and in vary-
ing degrees tolerates discrimination or even persecution. Much of the root
of this, in European Protestantism, Tillich saw in the Lutheran social
ethic, which is tolerant of many shades of totalitarian thought in the state
as long as the church as a bearer of "pure doctrine" is unmolested. In his
manuscript on "Protestantism and Anti-Semitism," Tillich writes, "there
is no guidance for politics in the Lutheran system." He argued that there
is less anti-Semitism in America than in Europe, not only because of the
religious pluralism found here but also because of the sectarian emphasis
of the presence of the divine in every human soul. In this "inner light"
mentality, every person is more important than an individual creed, and
the Jew is on equal footing with the Christian. For his own part, Tillich
rejected any notion of a Christian mission to the Jews, and in fact he felt
that the prophetic spirit of Judaism needs to be independently preserved
as a corrective to Christian churches, which so frequently border on
paganism.

Concerning the nation of Israel and the Zionist movement, Tillich
acknowledged that he had come to feel that any historically relevant
group had to make space for itself. It is therefore understandable that the
Jews need a land. The tension of modern Judaism, as indeed with the
biblical period, is between the land (sacred space) and a faith in the Holy
(being a people of a sacred time). The average Jew needs the identity of
space (the nation Israel), but not all Jews will be bearers of the exclusive
monotheism that points to the transhistorical Kingdom of God.

The basis for unity that Tillich saw in Judaism and in Christianity
was in the shared prophetic tradition and in a common mystical awareness of the Divine. Tillich felt that Kabbala mysticism had intertwined
with Jacob Böhme and hence entered into Christendom, and even
Bedyaev was influenced by Kabbalistic elements. Any movement for
religious renewal that affirms the mystical presence of the Divine can
potentially bring Jews and Christians closer together.

(3) *Psychotherapy and Personality.* Tillich's published works in this
area are, of course, extensive, and it is not surprising that a number of his
unpublished lecture notes are similar to his published work (for example,
his manuscript on "Psychiatry and Theology," presented to a theological
discussion group in Washington, D.C., in 1956). Tillich did, however, pay
a special tribute to Freud in a lecture given at the University of Minneso-
ta in 1957; he praised the rigor of Freud's naturalistic critique of religion

and of Freud's theory of culture, and he felt that Freud's work on the unconscious was of major significance for contemporary thought. On the critical side, however, he felt that Freud overstressed the libido and showed little sophistication about the meaning and function of religious symbols. The deepest human need, Tillich observed, is not for an analyst's acceptance but for a transcendent acceptance.

One undated and undesignated Tillich lecture was given at a conference for dialogue between Eastern and Western religious traditions. Tillich's typed notes on the topic "Immortality and Eternal Life" show how he contrasted two motifs. The religious issue, he argued, is in the search for continuing self-consciousness; both "immortality" and "eternal life" are symbols that point to this and attempt to make the notion vivid. Tillich felt that the philosophical clue is in the concept of essence; we can speak of a person's "essentialization" as a free actualization and hence as a continuous creation. Tillich wrote:

> Essentialization in this sense is not a simple return to what was, but a return with higher (or lower) fulfillment of our potentialities. This allows for a nonsuperstitious speaking of the eternal dimension of the soul and the belongingness of the body to the whole of being. Socrates' body is essentialized as much as his soul.

This quotation is typically Tillichian in language and is enigmatic, but it does show how Tillich within his own system was trying to build bridges between East and West.

Tillich's interest in human growth and dynamics is reflected in his talk entitled "On Creative Listening," which he gave at Bucknell University on the occasion of receiving an honorary degree. (This manuscript is typed and in semifinished format, but is undated.) No one can be creative, he maintains, who has not mastered the art of listening. To be a creative listener one must be willing to be drawn into subject matter. There is a hidden sublimity in the natural as well as the human realm, and the person with "ears to hear" can also become attuned to the unconscious depths of life. To be "depthful" people we do not need so much the stimulation or inspiration of others as we need the almost mystical sensitivity to the world about us and a responsibility for what one hears. And in the personal realm, Tillich observes:

> Creative listening to another person begins when silence has become possible between two people—the most difficult thing—and when

through this silence somebody speaks to us silently, and we listen so that a real communion is created. But it is not only the moment of mutual silence in which creative listening can take place, it is also within a seemingly superficial conversation in which one may hear many more things than are actually said. Hearing what the other *wants* to say, but is unable to, is creative listening. The more you are capable of doing this, the more precious human relations you will have.

Other materials in the Harvard collection include the handwritten versions of most of Tillich's English-language books (*Series E*), files of his early personal correspondence, his English professional correspondence from 1933 to 1965, and assorted memorabilia (for example, some photographs of his army days in World War I, some early German school notebooks, certificates, and awards).

Not all of the material at Harvard, however, is available. The Tillich Estate (of which Robert C. Kimball of the Starr-King School of Theology in Berkeley, California is literary executor) has "flagged" most of the manuscripts that are in near-finished form, presumably because of the possibility of their eventual publication. (These manuscripts can be read with permission of the Harvard librarian but cannot be photocopied or quoted without permission of the Tillich Estate.) The Estate has flagged much of Tillich's personal correspondence, including his correspondence with his family. It is my understanding that this material will not be made available to the public for fifty years. There is an ample amount of memorabilia from Tillich's early life, however, to give a distinct flavor to the man and his career, and extensive professional correspondence is readily accessible.

Some of Tillich's occasional newsletters to his friends around the world give insights into the vigorous professional pace he maintained. The following excerpt of his letter of February 1959, written from Cambridge, shows something of the pace of his work schedule.

The months before Christmas were filled with an unusual amount of regular work in Harvard (because of the absence of three members of our "Systematic" department) and with very important outside lectureships, sermons, and articles to be written. There was no weekend before Christmas in which I could have sent "Season's Greetings" to anybody. One of the reasons was a special sermon I had to give in the Washington Cathedral on December 28th to a conference of the American Association for the Advancement of Science, an event that brings together thousands of scientists. The large Cathedral was completely filled. From Washington, I went directly to Chicago for a four-week program of seven regular lecture hours weekly and many special obligations. These four weeks in the center of the Middle West of the United States are very important for my work. They take place every second year, and I have as many friends there as I have in Cambridge or Hamburg. The return trip from Chicago was interrupted by two lectures with discussions and extra speeches, and an additional burden of anxiety about a lecture on "Art and Ultimate Reality" to be given in the Museum of Modern Art in New York. (It had to be done with slides—*Lichtbilder*). When I sat down to prepare it, an unexpected interruption occurred. There was a painter waiting for me, sent by *Time* Magazine, to make a portrait of me for one of their March covers. I had to sit for him in my office for five mornings without being able to read, write or even think. He did a very good job—but the time for work was gone. Finally, I gave my New York lecture. But already on the return train, two reporters, a man and a woman, joined me and started a four-day interrogation period for the article about me in the same issue of *Time*. Again, four days for work were gone, and yesterday I had to give my sermon in the University Church at Harvard.

The second part of the Paul Tillich Archives includes the chronological shelving of all of the German and English writings, including chapters in various anthologies, reprinted material, translations of his books into various languages, and book reviews. This arrangement greatly facilities locating articles in now-defunct or not widely circulated journals. The archive in recent years has acquired copies of secondary works and dissertations dealing with Tillich's thought, and these additions add considerably to the research value of the collections.

Although it is personally moving and professionally interesting to review the memorabilia and unpublished work of Tillich, I finished my perusals of the Harvard archives with the distinct impression that most everything of consequence that Tillich had to say as a theologian has found its way into print. I was interested to find that in his last years, Tillich frequently lectured on the theme of ethics. He had apparently more interest in this area than his limited publications (for example, *Morality and Beyond*) would suggest. He had the tendency, however, to take a basic conceptual orientation in ethics and rework it in a dozen lectures, all of which are essentially the same. Few preachers and teachers, however, have room to criticize Tillich on this score.

II.

Researchers may indeed find other materials that deserve reflection. Professor Durwood Foster of the Pacific School of Religion reported at the North American Paul Tillich Society meeting in Orlando in 1998 that he had come across a transcript of a dialogue between Martin Buber and Tillich that was sponsored by Columbia University in the 1930s. There are notes from Tillich's Chicago years (1962–1965) related to his seminar with Mircea Eliade, but most of that seems to have been incorporated into his books *Christianity and the Encounter of the World Religions* and *The Future of Religions*.[4]

The Harvard archive welcomes visitors, and the dean's office at the Divinity School will assist scholars with housing.[5]

---

[4](New York: Columbia University Press, 1963) and (New York: Harper and Row, 1966), respectively.

[5][Editor's note.] Other primary research materials also are available to Tillich scholars in the form of audio tapes at the Paul Tillich Audio Tape Collection at Union Theological Seminary at Richmond. This collection is described as follows. "The Paul Tillich Collection, recorded over a thirteen-year period from 1952 to 1965, contains the full range of Paul Tillich's theological, religious, and philosophical thought. The tapes are arranged chronologically by year and series for reference and ordering, and are representative of the systematic development of Tillich's understanding of the Christian life. These tapes are not available for circulation, but are available for purchase."

As stated, the tapes are available for purchase, and for a reasonable fee one may hear again important lectures, addresses, sermons, and talks in Tillich's own voice. (The last tape in the collection is of the Tillich memorial service.) The list of tapes and ordering information appears online at <http://learn.union-psce.edu/resources/Media%20Center/tapes.htm>, or by e-mail at <medctr@union-psce.edu>.

The Paul Tillich Audio Tape Collection is housed at the Media Resource Center, a department of the William Smith Morton Library of the Union Theological Seminary and Presbyterian School of Christian Education, Richmond, Virginia.

Appendix B

THE PAUL TILLICH ARCHIVE AT THE UNIVERSITY OF MARBURG AND GERMAN TILLICH SCHOLARSHIP

Thanks to a grant from the German Academic Exchange Service (Deutscher Akademischer Austauschdienst, DAAD), I spent ten days in Marburg in 1980 working in the Paul Tillich Archive in the university library. I renewed my ties with the archive again while in Germany in the summer of 1998. The Tillich materials, carefully brought together and administered for many years by Frau Gertraut Stöber in Göttingen, were moved to the University of Marburg in the 1970s and have been supervised by the associate librarian in charge of archive materials and rare books, Dr. Uwe Bredehorn.

The accumulated materials in Marburg are roughly a European counterpart to the Paul Tillich Archives at Harvard. Most of Tillich's original manuscripts are in fact at Harvard; one project of the Marburg archive has been to obtain copies of those Harvard manuscripts. Even the originals of most of Tillich's early German writings are at Harvard but they have been copied on microfilm and are now available in Marburg as well.

Beginning in the early 1970s, however, many previously unknown Tillich works have been published in Germany as volumes in the series, *Ergänzungs- und Nachlassbände zu den Gesammelten Werken von Paul Tillich,* supplements and previously unpublished volumes to add to the collected works of Tillich. To date, twelve volumes of *Ergänzungs- und Nachlassbände* have appeared:

1–2. *Vorlesungen über die Geschichte des christlichen Denkens* (1971, 1972).
3. *An meine deutschen Freunde: die politischen Reden Paul Tillichs während des Zweiten Weltkriegs über die "Stimme Amerikas"; mit einer Einleitung und anmerkungen* (1973; [1]1971).
4. *Korrelationen: die Antworten der Religion auf Fragen der Zeit* (1971).

5. *Ein Lebensbild in Dokumenten: Briefe, Tagebuch-Auszüge, Berichte* (1971; n.s. 1980).

6. *Briefwechsel und Streitschriften: theologische, philosophische und politische Stellungnahmen und Gespräche* (1983).

7. *Frühe Predigten (1909–1918)* (1994).

8. *Vorlesung über Hegel (Frankfurt 1931/1932)* (1995).

9. *Frühe Werke* (1998, 1997).

10–11. *Religion, Kultur, Gesellschaft: unveröffentlichte Texts aus der deutschen Zeit (1908–1933)* (1999).

12. *Berliner Vorlesungen* (2001).[1]

Now also available is a six-volume condensation (or distillation) of the out-of-print, fourteen-volume *Gesammelte Werke*, in a German-English series entitled "Main Works/Hauptwerke," in which German works appear in German and English works in English. These six volumes are as follows.

1. *Philosophical Writings / Philosophische Schriften* (1989).

2. *Writings in the Philosophy of Culture / Kulturphilosophische Schriften* (1990).

3. *Writings in Social Philosophy and Ethics / Sozialphilosophische und ethische Schriften* (1998).

4. *Writings in the Philosophy of Religion / Religionsphilosophische Schriften* (1987).

5. *Writings on Religion / Religiöse Schriften* (1988).

6. *Theological Writings / Theologische Schriften* (1992).[2]

The creation of the Marburg archive was (and still is) a project of the German Paul Tillich Society (*Deutsche Paul-Tillich-Gesellschaft*). It was organized in 1960 by German friends of Paul Tillich. The location at the University of Marburg was urged by Professor Carl Heinz Ratschow, who

---

[1]Vols. 1–6 were published by Evangelisches Verlagswerk, Stuttgart and Frankfurt; vols. 7-12, by Walter de Gruyter, Berlin and New York.

[2]the Main Works/Hauptwerke series was published in Berlin and New York by de Gruyter and in Frankfurt and Berlin by Evangelisches Verlagswerk. The series was under the general editorial oversight of Carl Heinz Ratschow. Each volume also had its own individual editor, as follows (in order): Gunther Wenz, Michael F. Palmer, Erdmann Sturm, John Powell Clayton, Robert P. Scharlemann, and Gert Hummel.

was the first president of the German society and who held the old
Rudolf Otto chair in the History of Religions in the Marburg Protestant
Theological Faculty. There was also the historical tie that Tillich taught
at Marburg for three semesters in 1924–1925.[3] Primarily because of
Professor Ratschow, the University of Marburg was long recognized as
a center for Tillich studies in Germany. Professor Ratschow greeted me
warmly during my first visit to the archives, and I was assisted with all
of my inquiries by Dr. Bredehorn.

I was in Tübingen for an extended period before going to Marburg,
and my distinct impression from lectures, seminars, and informal
discussions there was that the German theological world is primarily
shaped these days by Barthian categories. Much to my surprise, I found
that the most popular theologian among Tübingen students was not
Jürgen Moltmann or Hans Küng but Eberhard Jungel, whose approach to
theology has been to reappraise the fundamental questions by way of
Barth and Luther. There is little doubt that the prevailing theological
ethos in Germany is molded by confessional and not philosophical
questions. Barth, therefore, as a church theologian is still "in," and Tillich
(in German circles juxtaposed to Barth in method and hermeneutics) is
seen as more of a philosopher of religion or as a theologian of culture.
What interest there is in Tillich, I have been advised, is more in the universities than in the churches. When one understands the general conservatism of the German churches, however, that is understandable.

I.

First, a few words about the organization of the Paul Tillich Archive
and the scope of its holdings. Not surprisingly, it is stronger on Tillich's
early German writings and lectures (that is, prior to 1933) and on the
unpublished lectures he gave at different German universities on his trips
back to Germany from 1948 to 1963. There has also been a major effort
to obtain a copy of every published work of Tillich's. Various spot-
checks satisfied me that the collection is essentially complete. The few
articles in English of which Frau Stöber could not get copies are available

---

[3]For a discussion of Tillich's Marburg years, see the Paucks' *Paul Tillich:
His Life and Thought* 1:94-98.

in German translation in the *Gesammelte Werke*, and they are easily tracked down through the *GW* index in volume 14.

The archive has had two different blocks of unpublished materials. The first group of materials was compiled by Frau Stöber over many years and contains early writings, remarks, lectures, handwritten outlines, sermons, letters, and even a few prayers written by Tillich for special occasions. These materials span the period from 1907 to 1963. Of special note for those interested in Tillich's early development are sixty-four sermons that he preached from 1909 to 1913, and 140 talks or sermons that he gave as a chaplain during the World War I. (The recent work of Professor Erdmann Sturm has probed the substance of these sermons, and I shall comment on his work later in this chapter.) Most of the ideas in the theological manuscripts—for example, "Das Problem der Geschichte: Das Unbedingtin die Geschichte"; "Die Krisis von Kultur und Religion"; "Religioser Sozialismus and Pazfismus," and so forth—were incorporated into later publications, so the Tillich scholar finds little new in these materials. This material has recently been published in volumes 7 and 9 of the *Ergänzungs- und Nachlassbände* series (see above), so the original documents are not now so unique.

The second group of unpublished materials was acquired from Frau Renate Albrecht, the indefatigable former student of Tillich's who was the editor of the *Gesammelte Werke*. Readers of this essay may not know that *GW* eventually grew to nineteen volumes of Tillich's works and included the formidable task of translating all of Tillich's English-language works back into German. Frau Albrecht has made available all of the drafts of the translations and all of the correspondence related thereto. Those papers, in fact, were still in suitcases on the library shelves when I first visited the archive in 1980. Such documents are undoubtedly important to have, but they do not exactly fire the imagination of scholars whose interests in Tillich area primarily theological. (I did, however, come across an interesting letter from Tillich to an editor complaining that after he had worked many hours with his translator he had concluded that volume 2 of his *Systematic Theology* was practically "untranslatable" into German!)

Two other features of the Marburg archives lend themselves to the classic American "good news/bad news" approach. The good news is that the archive contains extensive holdings of Tillichian secondary literature. In that way it differs from the Harvard archive. Much of this material (but not all) is catalogued alphabetically by author, and shelved chrono-logically according to the system devised by Frau Stöber. A part of this extensive collection includes microfilm copies of more than sixty American dissertations on Tillich and copies of some forty German dissertations. There are also copies of dissertations done in Italy, Spain, Holland, France, East Germany, and Czechoslovakia. The catalogue listings are supplemented by typed sheets of literature scanning done every six months since 1963 to identify other articles which have escaped previous researches. I recognized that even these periodical literature scans missed some things from the American scene, but even so it is very impressive to have in the archive such extended holdings of both primary and secondary Tillich scholarship.

Now the bad news. The Archive is located deep in the bowels of the university library and is accessible only when accompanied by Dr. Bredehorn. To get to the materials one goes through four locked doors, and Dr. Bredehorn has to press two switches before a large sliding shelf door opens and reveals the materials. All the materials are on two sets of facing shelves in the rare-book and archive stacks. Unfortunately there is no way of remaining with the materials just to browse unless Dr. Bredehorn is also present, and he is a very busy man. The method of working is to take the catalogue of indexed words to a library carrel, specify which works you want to see, and then Dr. Bredehorn personally retrieves them. It is not the easiest way to work with such diverse materials, especially with letters, pamphlets, and unbound writings. In this way it is a notable contrast to the Harvard archive, which has the Tillich materials in a large, well-lighted room with comfortable worktables. Everything there is easily accessible, and photocopying machines are close at hand. Security concerning the Marburg materials seems to be at a premium. In our computer age, however, specific requests for materials can be faxed to an inquirer.

II.

What about the interest in Tillich scholarship that has been going on in Germany? Clearly Tillich's contribution to theology is still a factor in the German intellectual scene because of the existence of the *Tillich Gesellschaft* and its annual meetings. The society selects a different theme for each annual meeting at Hofgeismar and invites papers on the theme. Discussion of the papers proceeds over a two- or three-day span. The

German society has a membership consisting of people from diverse academic backgrounds and professional interests. It is not surprising therefore that the themes of recent annual meetings have been interdisciplinary and dialogical. Topics for the six years 1994–1999 indicate the broad scope of the meetings.

> 1994. Hell und Heilen. Zum Gespräch zwischen Theologie, Medizin, und Psychotherapie.
> 1995. Fremde und Vertrautheit. Paul Tillich im Dialog mit einem Krisenphänomen unserer Zeit.
> 1996. Gott und das Böse. Zum Gespräch zwischen Theologie, Psychotherapie, Soziologie, und Pädagogik.
> 1997. Die Verlorene Lieblichkeit. Nach-demklichkeiten über ein Gegenswartsproblem in Umbreis der Theologie Paul Tillichs.
> 1998. Predigten mit fort-laufendum Erfolg! Brauchen wir ein neues religiöses Reden?
> 1999: Was ist der Mensch? Paul Tillichs Anthropologie im Dialog mit zeitgenössischen Fragen nach dem Wesen des Menschen.

In addition to the annual meetings of the *Deutsche Paul-Tillich-Gesellschaft* an International Paul Tillich Symposium is held every two years in Frankfurt am Main. These meetings have a much more academic/scientific character. Papers from all the symposiums have been published by Walter de Gruyter, among them the following: *God and Being* (1989); *New Creation or Eternal Now?* (1991); *Natural Theology versus Theology of Nature?* (1994); *The Theological Paradox* (1995); *Truth and History—a Dialogue With Paul Tillich* (1998); and *Being versus Word in Paul Tillich's Theology.*

During the 1990s, Professor Gert Hummel of the University of the Saarlandes served as president of the *Tillich Gesellschaft* and the focus of Tillich scholarship has shifted from Marburg to Saarbrücken. Hummel, who taught for a period of time at Capital University in Columbus, Ohio, is fluent in English and has been a link between the North American and German societies. (Professor Hummel retired from his academic post in 1998 and accepted a position as pastor to a German-speaking congregation in Tbilisi in the Republic of Georgia. He subsequently has been elected bishop of the Lutheran churches in that area of Georgia, but still commutes back to Germany and continues to serve as president of the *Tillich Gesellschaft*.) Professor Ratschow informed me that in the twenty-year span from 1960 to 1980 there had been more dissertations in systematic theology on Tillich in German universities than on any other single firgure. That concentration diminished in the 1990s, however, with the emergence of new theological streams and problems.

On scholarly fronts, Tillich scholarship in Germany over the past twenty years can be studied around two issues: (1) the debate over Tillich's life (and lifestyle) and its relationship to his thought; and (2) the renaissance of interest in Tillish's pre-World War I writings. I will comment on each of these in turn.

III.

The interest in Tillich's life and its relationship to his thought was precipitated by the publication of Hannah Tillich's book *From Time to Time*.[4] Why Hannah Tillich chose to write that book is an interesting story in its own right, but it lies beyond the scope of our interests here. Her book was eventually translated into German but that process was delayed considerably because the *Tillich Gesellschaft* threatened any German publisher of the book with a lawsuit. Many German friends of both Paulus and Hannah were deeply offended by her book and to this day have not forgiven her for writing it.

The next step in this controversy came in 1975 with the long-awaited biography of Marion Pauck and Wilhelm Pauck, *Paul Tillich: His Life and Thought*, volume 1. It was understood that this book was to be more or less the "authorized" biography of Tillich, and most Tillich scholars knew that it was nearly ten years in the making. Friends on both sides of the Atlantic waited to see how the Paucks would treat the delicate matter of the Tillich marriage and Tillich's pattern of relationships, as well as integrate the relationship of Tillich's life and thought. Although informative and bringing together many sources from Tillich's early years in Germany to which most Americans had no access, the Pauck volume drew sharp criticisms from both Americans and Germans. Its reception in America never quite recovered from the highly critical review by Gerald Brauer of the University of Chicago in *The Christian Century*.[5] Brauer faulted the authors for poor methodology in the use of interview

---

[4](New York: Stein and Day, 1973).

[5]See Brauer's "Tillich according to the Paucks," *The Christian Century* 93/3 (17 November 1976): 1017-20.

information. Knowledgeable people in Germany were taken aback by some errors of dates, places, and events which seemed to them to compromise the validity of the entire effort. Renate Albrecht was convinced that a reliable and balanced assessment of Tillich's life and thought would have to be done in Germany.

Against that background, three German books dealing with Tillich's life and thought are very interesting. One is a semipopular treatment in paperback by Gerhard Wehr entitled *Paul Tillich*.[6] It is enriched by many photographs of various other people and scenes in Germany and America to give some flavor of Tillich's *Sitz im Leben*. Wehr is a freelance writer who has done similar books on Martin Buber, Carl Jung, and Karl Barth. Methodologically he draws heavily on Tillich's own autobiological writings, quotes the Pauck volume three times, Rollo May once, and Hannah Tillich twice (but not from her critical passages). The "main themes" (*Elemente Theologischen Denkens*) are treated in twenty-two pages and the story of how the *Gesammelte Werke* came into being is told in four pages. Tillich's life story is told with no reference to the Hannah Tillich controversy.

The second volume was a more substantial work and a major publishing event. It appears as volume 5 in the new series of the *Gesammelte Werke*, and is entitled *Ein Lebensbild in Dokumenten: Briefe, Tagebuch-Auszüge, Berichte*.[7] Dividing Tillich's life into definable periods (childhood and youth; student days in Berlin, Tübingen, and Halle; vicar and assistant pastor; the First World War; war letters to Maria Klein (a student); marriage with Grete Wever; and so forth), the book fills out each chapter with primary documents: Tillich's own reflections and letters to friends; letters from friends and family; some apparently solicited remembrances from colleagues, Tillich's travel memoirs, and his summaries of activities that he had mimeographed and distributed to friends in Europe. (These are referred to as *Rundbriefe*.) There are indeed some fascinating glimpses into his life: his letters to his first wife, his impressions of his first week in New York, his reactions to his first visit back to Germany after World War II (in 1948), his impressions of Japan, the sadness of leaving Harvard, and many others.

---

[6](Hamburg: Rowohlt Taschenbuch Verlag, 1979).

[7]Ed. Ranate Albrecht and Margot Hahl (Stuttgart: Evangelisches Verlagswerk, 1980).

The book draws heavily on documents found in the Harvard and Marburg archives. In many ways it is a supplement and corrective to the Pauck volume, but it avoids the major controversies of the Hannah Tillich depiction of Paulus. Margot Hahl, one of the coeditors, contributed a remembrance of Paulus and Hannah which, while acknowledging that there were some tensions and ambivalence in the relationship, denies the Pauck evaluation that "the marriage was unhappy from its beginning" (Pauck, page 86). The detailed footnotes of this volume suggest that one major purpose was to correct the factual errors in the Pauck book (compare pages 25, 49-50, 73-74, 109-10, 141, 198).

A third German work on Tillich's life and thought is Carl Heinz Ratschow's essay that appeared in the collection *Theologen des Protestantismus im 19. und 20. Jahrhundert*.[8] This essay was translated by Robert P. Scharlemann and published in 1980 by the North American Paul Tillich Society as a slim (44 pages) monograph entitled simply *Paul Tillich*.[9] This essay chronicles Tillich's professional and intellectual history and argues that in his writings Tillich was able to transcend the problems of his time.[10] (This work, by the way, is still available through the NAPTS, and is an excellent volume for beginning students and laypersons.)

All of these studies reflect that Tillich's German friends (that is, those active in the *Tillich Gesellschaft*) either did not "see" (or fundamentally disagreed with) the shortcomings in Tillich the man which the Paucks discovered. For some in the Tillich circle in Germany, Tillich was practically comparable to Goethe in his profundity of thought and universality of interests, and for anyone to point to personal shortcomings

---

[8]Two volumes, ed. Matine Greschat, Urban Taschenbücher bd. 284-285 (Stuttgart and Berlin: Kohlhammer Verlag, 1978).

[9](Iowa City: University of Iowa Press for the NAPTS, 1980). The English translation was made from a copy of Prof. Ratschow's typescript and includes his complete bibliography and footnotes.

[10]See now also Bernd Jaspert and Carl Heinz Ratschow, *Paul Tillich: ein Leben für die Religion*, Didaskalia 32 (Kassel: Verlag Evangelischer Presseverband, 1987): "Die Neuentdeckung der Religion im 20. Jahrhundert—Das Lebenswerk Paul Tillich (1886–1965)" (Jaspert) and "Protestantisches Prinzip und religiöser Atheismus bei Paul Tillich" (Rathschow).

(vanity, ego, and the loss of prophetic consciousness) was regarded as petty and self-serving.

The second domain of recent Tillich scholarship in Germany relates to the renewed interest in Tillich's early (that is, pre-World War I) writings. This interest revolves around two foci: the research into Tillich's philosophical writings from 1906 to 1913, done primarily by Professor Gert Hummel and his assistant, Doris Lax; and the work done on Tillich's early sermons by Professor Erdmann Sturm of the University of Münster. The work by Hummel and Lax began when Hummel discovered some previously unknown handwritten manuscripts of Tillich's dated from 1906 to 1913. It turned out that these were written in an old German script called *Sütterlin*. *Sütterlin* was favored in the eastern provinces when Tillich was a boy, but it is difficult to decipher today, even for native German speakers.

Hummel turned the difficult task of translating Tillich's manuscripts to Ms. Lax, who in the process discovered that they included a complete version of a systematic theology. She published a critical edition of this work in her 1995 M.A. thesis at the University of Saarbrücken. This meant, of course, that Tillich's work on his *Systematic Theology* had taken shape ten years before most scholars thought he had begun working on this project. Ms. Lax has summarized the major themes of this 1913 systematic theology in an unpublished paper entitled "The Paradox: Principles and Method of Tillich's 1913 Systematic Theology," which she presented at a recent meeting of the French Tillich Society. This paper has been submitted to several prominent American journals and I am hopeful that it will soon appear for American readers.

Hummel and Lax included the full German text of the 1913 systematic theology in their edition of Tillich's *Frühe Werke*, volume 9 of the *Ergänzungs- und Nachlassbände* series.[11] The bad news is that this impressive volume of 600 pages (it includes several other of Tillich's early philosophical writings) costs more than $100.00. The good news is that this 1913 systematic theology has been translated by Uwe Carsten

---

[11]*Frühe Werke*, ed. Gert Hummel and Doris Lax, Ergänaungs- und Nachlassbände zu den Gesammelten Werken von Paul Tillich bd. 9 (Berlin and New York: Walter de Gruyter, 1998, 1997) viii+598 pages.

Scharf in his *The Paradoxical Breakthrough of Revelation*.[12] This also-quite-expensive volume is a revised version of Scharf's 1995 dissertation at the University of Virginia, done under the supervision of Robert Scharlemann and Langdon Gilkey. Scharf is a native German who emigrated to America and who now works as a clinical pastoral educator at the Duke University Medical Center. Probably only a native German could have translated this volume, and we are indebted to Scharf for his work. Readers will find in his 1913 systematic theology some of Tillich's earliest writings about Paradox, Kairos, and revelation. Further commentary would go beyond our space and interests here.

The second component of the renewed interest in Tillich's pre-World War I writings is found in the recent work of Erdmann Sturm, especially in his editing of the *Ergänzungs- und Nachlassbände* two volumes entitled *Religion, Kultur, Gesellschaft:. unveröffentliche Texte aus der deutschen Zeit (1908–1913)*.[13] Since most American and British scholars, when they have spoken of Tillich's early German writings, have been familiar only with Tillich's post-World War I writings, Sturm's work has exposed both German- and English-speaking scholars to a whole corpus of Tillich's earlier work in philosophy and culture. In 1906, for example, at age twenty, Tillich published a major essay comparing Fichte's philosophy to the theological framework of the Fourth Gospel. (That essay, by the way, is found in the new Hummel and Lax volume mentioned above.) Sturm also edited one of the six volumes of the Main Works/Hauptwerke series, *Writings in Social Philosophy and Ethics*.[14] This volume includes some hitherto unknown essays but also includes a number of essays that—thanks to James Luther Adams—are familiar to American scholars.

The most creative aspect of Sturm's work on Tillich, in my opinion, is related to the work he has done on Tillich's sermons while Tillich was a young vicar in the old Lutheran Church of Brandenberg. Tillich's father

---

[12]Subtitled *Interpreting the Divine-Human Interplay in Paul Tillich's Work, 1913–1964*, Theologische Bibliothek Töpelmann bd. 83 (Berlin and New York: Walter de Gruyter, 1999).

[13]Two volumes, Ergänzungs- und Nachlassbände zu den Gesammelten Werken von Paul Tillich 10-11 (Berlin and New York: Walter de Gruyter, 1999).

[14](German) *Sozialphilosophische und ethische Schriften*, Main Works/Haupt-werke vol./bd. 3 (Berlin and New York: Waler de Gruyter, 1998).

was a rather conservative official in that church. From the Marburg archives, Sturm received copies of sermons Tillich preached as a young vicar in several small towns in the province of Brandenberg from 1909 until he went into the army in 1914. Sturm has examined the motifs of those sermons, along with the themes of Tillich's war sermons, in a essay entitled "Between Apologetics and Pastoral Care: Tillich's Early Sermons." I have not seen the German version of this essay but I have reviewed a translation of the essay prepared by Doris Lax of the *Tillich Gesellschaft*.[15]

Sturm's assessment is that Tillich's early sermons vacillate between the two themes of apologetics and pastoral care. Even as a young vicar Tillich seemed to feel that it would be the task of educated people to develop a more sophisticated understanding of Christianity if the faith were to have appeal and relevance in the twentieth century. That of course was his apologetic interest. Tillich also was aware of the pains and need of human existence, and that moved him to incorporate themes of hope and promise into his sermons. (These observations are actually not so startling; I suspect most preachers in America today would identify with these two themes.)

Sturm thinks we can trace an evolution in Tillich's preaching from his 1908 probationary sermon (preached to the Royal Consistory, on 1 Corinthians 3:21-23, to qualify him as a licensed preacher) through the Lichtenrade sermons (1909) and the Nauen sermons of 1911–1912. By the time of the Nauen sermons Tillich seemed to move away from apologetics, and to stress more the mystical themes of communion with God and participation in eternity in time. Tillich seemed to feel that it is natural for humans to have a sense of melancholy in view of our finiteness, but we can also be certain that the Divine love is eternal love. We can hence live with confidence. (It is of course interesting to note how this same theme is later expressed in different language in his *Systematic Theology*.)

---

[15]"Zwischen Apologetik und Seelsorge. Paul Tillichs frühe Predigten (1908–1918)," *Theologische Literaturzeitung* 124 (1999): 251-68; and see "Between Apologetics and Pastoral Care: Paul Tillich's Early Sermons (1908–1918)," in the *North American Paul Tillich Society Newsletter* 26/1 (2000).

The limited space of this chapter requires I not elaborate more specifically on Tillich's pre-World War I sermons, but I do want to comment on Sturm's assessment of Tillilch's war sermons in the trenches as a young chaplain in the German army. Sturm uncovered directives from the German general staff that chaplains were not to speak of military or political matters in sermons unless their comments were in favor of military and political leaders. It was understood (not surprisingly) to be the task of chaplains to speak out against "murmuring" and discontent among the troops, to interpret defeats theologically, to be a pastoral presence amid death and dying, and to interpret suffering and death theologically—that is, as "sacrificial" deaths for the Fatherland. To do this Tillich used a lot of texts from the Old Testament, and frequently compared the plight of German soldiers to the situation of the Israelites in conducting a "holy war." From the standpoint of eighty-five years later and from the perspective of a non-German, the recurring themes of the war sermons seem too nationalistic, but in all fairness we have to recognize that Tillich was in a difficult position and probably was doing the best he could do under the circumstances. Any chaplain who publically questioned the rightness of the war or of Germany's cause would have been instantly removed or shot. Some of Tillich's letters to his family reveal, however, his own despair and horror at what he had seen. Surely we can say that Tillich in 1914–1918 had no idea his exhortations to German troops would be read by anyone eighty-five years later, and read in an entirely different context.

Sturm also analyzes some of the sermons Tillich preached at Spandau (a suburb of Berlin, which included a hospital and the famous military prison) in the fall of 1918 where he was assigned after the war. Here he repeatedly said that this is going to be a time for rebuilding and for the formation of a new kind of church. (We see in these sermons some hints of his later interpretation of the church as "spiritual presence" that he develops fully in the final version of his *Systematic Theology*, volume 3.)

Space concerns prevent further commentary on the significance these early sermons, but suffice it to say that Sturm's work breaks much new ground in our understanding of Tillich as Christian and pastor prior to 1920. From Sturm's work we catch a glimpse of Tillich as a minister, and the interests of ministers are often quite different from the interests of theologians. I look forward to the appearance of Sturm's work in the United States. Most scholars have had keener interest in the early Tillich as a philosopher and social critic than they have had in Tillich as a Christian pastor.

IV.

There are, of course, other continuing studies being done on Tillich in Germany, but I do not have space here to discuss recent monographs and dissertations. Many of the better dissertations of the past twenty years have been translated into English and are well known by Tillich scholars. Information about newer studies can be obtained by e-mail correspondence directly with the Tillich archive in Marburg or through the *Deutsche Paul-Tillich-Gesellschaft*, whose e-mail address is <Niewerth@t-online.de>.

Almost all of Tillich's writings from his American period have been translated into German, and many, including the *Systematic Theology*, are still in print. The corpus of the six-volume Main Works/Hauptwerke and the *GW* supplemental series is available in virtually all seminary and major research university libraries. New interpretive books on Tillich are mentioned on the internet homepage of the *Deutsche Paul-Tillich-Gesellschaft*, at <http://www.uni-trier.de/uni/theo/tillich.html>.

I conclude this chapter with the sad report that the two women who did more than anyone else to collect and edit the German works of Paul Tillich have recently died. Renate Albrecht died in 1995 and Gertraut Stöber died in 1997 at age ninety-one. I dedicated *Kairos and Logos* (1978, 1984) to them, and once again I want to recognize their outstanding work. All Tillich scholars are in their debt.

Appendix C

THE NORTH AMERICAN PAUL TILLICH SOCIETY: WHENCE AND WHITHER?[1]

Although I met Paul Tillich in 1955 at Union Theological Seminary in New York and hosted him when he lectured at Florida State University in 1962, I was not a formal student of his, nor was I one of those who served as his assistants. In previous years we have invited people to speak at our banquet who either worked with Paulus or knew him personally. Like many others, I have learned much from the banquet reflections of Marion Pauck, John Dillenberger, James Luther Adams, Krister Stendahl, Durwood Foster, Tom Driver, and Langdon Gilkey. All these "eyewitnesses" have enriched our sense of Tillich's scholarly work, his habits and life patterns, and his relationship with colleagues. My own modest contribution to Tillich scholarship, however, is related much more to the founding of the North American Paul Tillich Society (NAPTS) and in helping to get our publication series started with Mercer University Press.

In my remarks I want to do four things: (1) comment on what went into the first consultation on Tillich Studies in 1974, and on the formation of the Society in 1975; (2) share some reflections on the evolution of the Society; (3) include a few recollections of my times with Tillich when he came to give a lecture at Florida State University in 1962; and (4) comment on three ways Tillich has impacted on my entire professional career.

I.

Let me begin by recounting what went into the calling of the first consultation on Tillich studies in 1974. From 1972 to 1978, when I was

---

[1]This is essentially my banquet address to the 1998 annual meeting of the North American Paul Tillich Society in Orlando, Florida, in November.

chair of the Religion Department at Florida State University, the national office of the American Academy of Religion (AAR) was also at Florida State. John Priest and Bob Spivey served as executive directors of the AAR during that period. Although in some ways this office was semi-independent from the work of our department, all of us there knew what was going on in the planning of the AAR activities, and we were briefed regularly about the shaping of the AAR program.

It dawned on me one day in early 1974, that in spite of Tillich's wide influence there had never been special consultation on the status of Tillich studies. I discussed this with John Priest, my colleague who was serving as executive director of the AAR at that time, and he agreed it would be timely to include such a consultation on the program. As I remember, we did not have to get approval for this from a national committee of thirty-five; Priest just said, "It's a good idea and let's do it." I told him I would be responsible for planning the consultation. I got in touch with James Luther Adams to get his advice and counsel about how to use that time profitably. He suggested I contact the *Deutsche Paul-Tillich-Gesellschaft* to include, if possible, a report on European Tillich scholarship. He also gave me the names of a number of people he had been in touch with (many being former students of his) who he thought would be interested in attending a consultation on Tillich studies.

About seventy-five people attended that first consultation, which was held in one three-hour block of time at the Washington Hilton. It was clear, after some group discussion, that there was an interest in creating a more formal structure for Tillich scholarship. It was agreed that a steering committee should draft a constitution and bylaws, and we would consider those at the 1975 AAR meeting in Chicago. Jack Boozer of Emory, Bob Scharleman (then at the University of Iowa), Peter John, and I constituted a committee for the preparation of the constitution and bylaws.

The first consultation included, among other things, a major address by James Luther Adams; a report on the history and work of the German Tillich society; a report on recent dissertations in Tillich studies; several papers presented as works in progress; and a business meeting. The consultation helped Tillich scholars meet each other, and we developed a mailing list of people who were present at the consultation for future newsletters related to Tillich scholarship. (As I recall there was some revival of interest of Tillich and his work sparked by the publication in

1973 of Hannah Tillich's book, *From Time to Time*.) We also agreed that we should undertake the task of publishing essays of current Tillich scholarship.

About 100 people attended the organizational meeting of the society in Chicago in 1975. For that meeting, I prepared a small book entitled *Tillich Studies: 1975*, which included contributions from John Dourley from Carleton University in Ottawa, Canada, Roy Morrison from Wesley Theological Seminary, Jim Fisher from Bentley College in Massachusetts, Walter Bense from University of Wisconsin in OshKosh, Ronald Stone from Pittsburgh Theological Seminary, John Lounibos from the Domican College of Blauvelt, New York, Paul Wiebe of Witchita State University, and H. Fred Reisz, Jr. (then at Wittenburg University in Springfield, Ohio). That collection of essays gave those who attended the founding meeting a sense of the range and scope of interpretative Tillich scholarship.

The fact that the headquarters of the AAR was located at Florida State likewise helped us in this organizational meeting. The long-awaited and much-talked-about Pauck volume on Tillich had just been published, and I was able to persuade John Priest that Wilhelm Pauck would be a good plenary speaker for one of the AAR evening sessions. That in fact was worked out, and Pauck was invited. A crowd of somewhere between 800 to 1,000 heard Paulk reflect about Tillich and his experiences with him. That plenary session supplemented well the interest in Tillich that the founding of our society created. It was at the Chicago meeting that we approved a constitution and bylaws, and endorsed our present structure of officers and board of directors for the Society.

Active and influential in those early deliberations were Bob Scharlemann, Guy Hammond of Virginia Tech, Ray Bulman of St. John's University in New York City, Victor Nuovo of Middlebury College, Jack Boozer of Emory, Fred Reisz, Jr., Ron Stone of Pittsburg Theological Seminary, Mary Ann Stenger of Louisville, Arnold Wettstein of Rollins College, Tom O'Meara of Notre Dame and Peter John. We began the process of preparing and circulating a newsletter, which was the responsibility of the secretary/treasurer. I served as the first president, Victor Nuovo was the first vice-president, and Peter H. John was the first secretary/treasurer.

(Old-time Tillich scholars will recall that Peter H. John was a New England United Methodist pastor. Peter John was well known as the one who followed Tillich to most of his speaking engagements, and he recorded many of Tillich's speeches in shorthand. He was really Tillich's Boswell! It was from his original shorthand notes on Tillich's spring 1953 course on the "History of Christian Thought" at Union Theological Seminary in New York that we have the manuscript that was edited and revised to become *A History of Christian Thought*.[2] I have lost touch with Peter John, but in the early days of the Society he was something of a legend for his reputation as one who preserved so many of Tillich's lectures. Tillich, by the way, did not particularly appreciate what Peter John was doing, but Peter nevertheless persisted in this task.)

II.

The 1998 meeting of the Society—at which this banquet address was presented—marked the twenty-third anniversary of the founding of the NAPTS; 2000 of course was the quarter-century mark. We have matured over the years, and many of those people active in the beginning have retired or moved on to different arenas of scholarship. The Society has grown far beyond our original vision. It has also been satisfying to see a new generation of Tillich scholars emerge and to recognize that our programming in the Society has become more internationalized. Some of that internationalization, of course, is related to the important work that Jean Richard has done in Canada. We have heard papers from scholars from the United Kingdom, Northern Ireland, Germany, Luxembourg, Norway, Belgium, and Latin America. We have had several joint meetings with the German Paul Tillich Society. We held an international meeting in Quebec, and special meetings such as the one in Atlanta in 1986 (commemorating the centennial of Tillich's birth) and the special

---

[2][Editor's note.] Peter John published these transcripts privately, in 1953 and 1956 (rev. ed.). This encouraged another Tillich "editor," Carl E. Braaten, to reedit and introduce the transcripts for what has become the best-known and most-popular edition of *A History of Christian Thought* (1960, [2]1968). No doubt it was the same original Tillich "Boswell" who encouraged Braaten later to edit and introduce (from a transcription of audio tapes) Tillich's spring 1963 lectures at the Divinity School, University of Chicago, published in 1967 as *Perspectives on 19th and 20th Century Theology*.

international meetings in New Harmony, Indiana, in the summer of 1993 and 1999.

Let me share three other observations about the work of the Society. The first is that in addition to our regular meetings, we have been a conduit for the publication of Tillich studies and research. In association with the Society, Mercer University Press has published *Kairos and Logos* (1984), *Theonomy and Autonomy* (1984), and *Being and Doing* (1987). Mercer University Press also published J. Mark Thomas's edited volume of Tillich's writings entitled *The Spiritual Situation in Our Technical Society* (1988); this work is a thematic organization of Tillich's essays dealing with religion, science, and technology in both his German and American periods. In addition to the publications by Mercer University Press, Bob Scharleman inaugurated a great service for us when he established the practice of publishing papers that are presented at our annual meeting, and Fred Parella has continued that tradition. Some of those papers have been reprinted in other publications as well, but they at least have given members of the Society a way to keep abreast of the current edges of Tillich scholarship.

A second observation is to remind us that the Society has many more members than those who are able to attend annual meetings. Part of Tillich's charisma during his lifetime, of course, was his ability to appeal to "the educated layman" and to people of diverse professional backgrounds. We have had members of the Society from the medical professions, engineering, law, journalism, and various other academic and professional disciplines. This is to remind us that the society has both a technical and a generalized membership, and we need to be aware that there is always a larger audience interested in ongoing Tillich scholarship than only those who gather at our annual meeting.

A third observation is that as a Society we owe much to the continuing interest and support of Mrs. Jane Owen and the Blaffer Trust. Not only did she invite us and welcome us to New Harmony, Indiana in 1993 and 1999, but the Blaffer Trust has provided financial assistance for our publishing ventures, for example, with Mercer University Press. We are indebted to her for her interest and support of the Society.

III.

Let me share a few memories of my time with Tillich in Tallahassee in 1962, and then comment briefly on the debts I owe to Paulus in my own professional development. I served as his host for the three days he was at Florida State University. On his first night a colleague of mine, Jackson Ice, and I took him to dinner at a local restaurant. When it came time to order dessert, he told the waitress that he would have jello. Jack and I looked at each other with some amazement, and I asked him why he ordered jello when there were some other Southern goodies on the menu like Florida key lime pie and pecan pie. He replied that he always ate jello for dessert when he could, because when he was a young boy his mother had told him that jello was good for the mind. Since that time thirty-six years ago, I have become a more serious jello-eater, but unfortunately have not noticed much improvement in my intellectual abilities. That evening before we went onstage for his lecture, we were standing backstage and he looked up and saw some of the ropes and pulleys that controlled the curtains of the main stage. He studied them for a minute or two and then told me that he thought they symbolized the demonic. "Holy Smoke!" I thought. "He never eases up!"

I also recall talking with him about how it felt to be the subject of so many doctoral dissertations. "It is very interesting," he said. "I always learn a lot from those dissertations. These young scholars always speak about what sources I was drawing upon, and what subtle themes I had in mind. Most of the time I can't recall thinking about any of those themes when I was writing!"

On a more serious note, I also remember from his Tallahassee visit his willingness to meet for a two-hour discussion session with about 200 students and faculty members in a large university lounge on a Saturday morning. The questions that were asked were probably typical of what undergraduate students ask. He treated each question, however, with great seriousness and often linked a rather ordinary question with some great philosophical issue. It was a classic example of a master teacher conveying to an audience that there is no such thing as an inappropriate question. The lecture that he gave at Florida State was entitled "Ethical Principles of Moral Action"; I included this as an appendix in the 1986 volume entitled *Being and Doing*. He was one of four speakers that I know of in the history of Florida State University who filled the main auditorium, which seats more than 3,000 people. (The others, incidentally, were Hans Küng, Abraham Heschel, and Elie Wiesel.)

IV.

Let me conclude by commenting on three ways Tillich's work has guided me in the course of my own academic career.

1. I was drawn to Tillich relatively late in my formal education. Other than getting a brief introduction to him in a class on contemporary theology taught by Claude Welch when I was at the Yale Divinity School, I did not do much reading in Tillich when I was there. In fact, the concentration of my work at that time was in the biblical field. I turned to Tillich more and more, however, when early in my career as a college and university chaplain, I moved from a small church-related college to Florida State University. Florida State was, and is, a typical large state institution. I quickly came to realize that the framing of issues of faith and learning took many forms, and that most of them could not be easily transposed into biblical categories. I was drawn to Tillich in an attempt to find new vocabularies. As I read more I was moved by Tillich's ability to be a "bridge builder" to many other academic disciplines. I remember talking with George Buttrick when he made a visit to Florida State while he was still at the Harvard Memorial Church. Buttrick said he thought Tillich could "build a bridge" to anybody.

In that state university setting I found Tillich to be enormously helpful with his broader interests in depth psychology, health, art, philosophy, and culture. He helped me see that biblical concerns can indeed be expressed through other vocabularies, and hence gave me a place to stand amid the din of voices in a large state institution. When I returned to Duke for my Ph.D. program I knew I wanted to write a dissertation on Tillich.

2. Secondly, I recall being deeply moved when I read in his comments about faith and doubt in the preface of *The Protestant Era*. Like most young scholars I lived rather precariously on the boundary of faith and doubt. Tillich reminded his readers of an insight that he came to early in his career, namely, that if the doctrine of justification by faith applies to us in spite of our sin, then it also applies to us in spite of our doubt. He noted in that preface that "without this realization I could not have remained a theologian." That passing observation shifted my sense of the task of theology and made me realize that we are not saved by having correct theologies. To understand all theological systems as incomplete and symbolic efforts to articulate what may be beyond human

speech was a changing awareness for me of the whole theological task of Christendom. This insight seems commonplace now, but it was liberating to me when I was a young scholar.

3. Thirdly, Tillich exemplified for me how a theologian can and should have wider intellectual interests. His work in science and religion, his interests in art forms, his early assessment of political issues, his juxtaposition of the Protestant Principle with Catholic Substance, and his famous observation that "culture is the essence of religion, and religion the form of culture," all stretched me to think about problems beyond biblical categories. Of course I learned much from the reading of *The Systematic Theology*, and still go back to it periodically to see how he interpreted different issues. But somehow with his work on the diverse aspects of culture, and his willingness to address a wide theological agenda both inspired me and enabled me to remain in the Christian tradition. I suspect everyone now reading these words has his or her own special debt to Tillich that could be added to these that I have shared.

[Editor's note. Professor Carey closed his November 1998 banquet address at the annual meeting of the NAPTS with the following personal observations, which seem appropriate still, especially for younger and would-be Tillichians.]

V.

The invitation to be the banquet speaker this year coincides with my retirement from professional academic life. I will be retiring from Agnes Scott this coming December 31 after forty-two years in academic work, and will be relocating to our home in Tallahassee, Florida. I hope, however, to remain active with the Society, and I want to encourage younger members to carry on with the work of the Society. I am mindful, of course, that theological issues come and go, and that theologians take turns at being in and out of the spotlight. I think that one measure of Tillich's greatness was to identify and struggle with these recurring problems of theology and philosophy—issues of life, death, and destiny. I would say of Tillich what he said of Marx, namely, that the questions he asked were so important, that it doesn't matter if his answers need revising. I still think that Paul Tillich is a man for all seasons, and I am grateful for this Society which enables us to further his thought and his spirit. I am sure that a younger generation of Tillich scholars will continue to find in Paulus rich sources to explore, and that for them, as well as for us, he will be a light along the way.

Index